THE BATTLE CRY OF THE
Siamese Kitten

Also by Philipp Schott

The Accidental Veterinarian
The Willow Wren
How to Examine a Wolverine
Fifty-Four Pigs

THE BATTLE CRY OF THE
Siamese Kitten

EVEN MORE TALES FROM THE
ACCIDENTAL VETERINARIAN

Philipp Schott DVM

Published by ECW Press
665 Gerrard Street East
Toronto, Ontario, Canada M4M 1Y2
416-694-3348 / info@ecwpress.com

Cover design: David A. Gee
Interior illustrations: Brian Gable

LIBRARY AND ARCHIVES CANADA
CATALOGUING IN PUBLICATION

Title: The battle cry of the Siamese kitten:
even more tales from the accidental
veterinarian / Philipp Schott DVM.

Names: Schott, Philipp, author.

Identifiers: Canadiana (print) 20220188637 |
Canadiana (ebook) 20220188653

ISBN 978-1-77041-669-7 (softcover)
ISBN 978-1-77852-032-7 (ePub)
ISBN 978-1-77852-033-4 (PDF)
ISBN 978-1-77852-034-1 (Kindle)

Subjects: LCSH: Veterinary medicine—
Anecdotes. | LCSH: Pets—Anecdotes.
| LCSH: Schott, Philipp. | LCSH:
Veterinarians—Manitoba—Biography.
| LCGFT: Anecdotes. | LCGFT:
Autobiographies.

Classification: LCC SF745 .S36 2022
| DDC 636.089—dc23

This book is funded in part by the Government of Canada. *Ce livre est financé en partie par le
gouvernement du Canada.* We acknowledge the support of the Canada Council for the Arts. *Nous
remercions le Conseil des arts du Canada de son soutien.* We acknowledge the support of the
Ontario Arts Council (OAC), an agency of the Government of Ontario, which last year funded 1,965
individual artists and 1,152 organizations in 197 communities across Ontario for a total of $51.9
million. We also acknowledge the support of the Government of Ontario through Ontario Creates.

PRINTED AND BOUND IN CANADA   PRINTING: MARQUIS   5 4 3 2 1

For Nico & Alex.
They love all Siamese kittens,
no matter how wild.

CONTENTS

PREFACE

Here we are again. Or at least, here I am again. I suppose this could be your first time picking up one of my books. Either way, welcome or welcome back, and thank you.

And if it is your first time, don't be afraid. You don't need to read the books, or even the tales within them, in order as they don't build on each other. Each tale is a discrete self-contained unit, like a snack, rather than an ingredient meant to be blended. Most other books are grand multi-course meals, whereas I like to think of my three veterinary books as collections of story snacks, or tapas if you prefer.

You have 60 tiny plates in front of you (and about 120 more in the other books — think of them as adjacent tables, easily within reach if you stretch a bit). They are laid out left to right but pick them up as you please. Eat them all in one sitting, or one per day, or ten per weekend, or at entirely random and wanton intervals.

When I began writing the first book, *The Accidental Veterinarian*, I briefly considered trying to weave the stories into a continuous narrative, like a traditional book. Many of the individual stories already existed as blog posts, so I would have to write some sort of filler to connect them. "Filler" sounds pejorative, doesn't it? I don't mean it that way. The filler might have been beautiful and engaging, but it would have been false. I'm blessed with a good memory, but not an unnaturally good one that allows me to conjure up the level of detail needed to turn all these stories into a smooth continuum. I did exactly that with *The Willow Wren*, the fictionalized memoir of my father growing up during the rise and fall of Hitler's Germany (yes, that was shameless plug for an unrelated book), and there the filler worked, but it didn't feel right for my veterinary stories. Moreover I thought that there might be a place in the modern reader's library for collections of story snacks. I hope I am right.

In the spirit of story snacking, I've done away with the sections in this volume. *The Accidental Veterinarian* and *How to Examine a Wolverine* were divided into four sections each, roughly grouping stories by type — sort of thematically in the first book and sort of by species in the second. But for a significant number of stories, these categorizations felt arbitrary. Here the snack metaphor breaks down. Until they start making sweet chips, salty fruit, or crunchy cheese, it's fairly easy to group snacks. Veterinary stories, not so much.

So, here you will have them presented alphabetically, which is as close to random as my relentlessly systemizing brain will permit. But feel free to proceed as your heart dictates.

And again, welcome, or welcome back. And again, thank you. Thank you so much.

AFFENPINSCHER TO ZWERGPINSCHER

A picture exists of me at about six months of age being shown a black-and-white dairy cow. My father and I are on a snow-dusted country lane outside of Jülich, in western Germany, where I was born. The lane runs beside a fenced field. Everything is flat and barren and cold-looking, but there is this cow as the singular object of interest. My father is holding me out towards the fence. The cow is craning its neck towards me, but I am looking sideways at the camera and my mother, who is taking the picture. My facial expression is one of pure astonishment. My eyes are wide and my mouth open round like a big O. This was likely the largest animal I had ever seen.

That was the first picture of me with an animal. Later ones in my toddler years, by then in Saskatoon, show me trying awkwardly to pet a random outdoor cat while wearing a Michelin Man snowsuit and feeding old rubbery carrots to the deer at the local zoo. Back then nobody, including the zookeepers, thought this might be a bad idea.

So those were my earliest documented encounters with animals. My earliest clear memory of an animal, however, is of my cousin's dog, a black cocker spaniel named Tino. This would have been the early 1970s, and I might have been five or seven years old. As I explained in *The Accidental*

Veterinarian, there was no way I was going to have a dog or a cat. My parents didn't actively dislike them, but it was just that pets simply weren't part of their world, any more than watching pro sports was, or eating Jell-O, peanut butter, or marshmallows. These were things other people did, and that was fine, but it just didn't interest them. This would eventually change, but not until much later (and never for the marshmallows or pro sports).

But somehow the interest in animals was there. Was it genetic? My father was passionate about birds and impressed me when they landed on his outstretched hand. He claimed that, according to German legend, because he was born on a Sunday, he had the gift of being able to talk to birds. (What special powers being born on a Saturday might have granted me were never explained.) But rather than genetics, I think it might have been because from a young age I read like a threshing machine. I quickly exhausted the children's section of the small local J.S. Wood branch of the library. I remember the day clearly when my mother suggested that I have a look at the teen and young adult section instead. I began with the letter "A" on the non-fiction shelves and worked my way through. (Yes, I was an odd child, and a self-confident one, which is an unusual combination and explains a lot about me. But never mind that.) "D" was a gold mine, encompassing both dinosaurs and dogs. In retrospect I realize the library likely didn't have any cat books. Otherwise, my abstract affection might have alighted on them. But as it was, the J.S. Wood had a gorgeously illustrated dog breed guidebook. It was so orderly and alphabetical. I was captivated.

And there, in that book, was a picture of my cousin's dog, Tino. Or at least a dead ringer for him. Glossy black fur, long silky ears, warm brown eyes looking right at me from the page. From that point on, in the weird logic of the small child, Tino, although I had only met him once, became "my dog" in my mind and my heart. And that logic truly was weird because not only had I only met

Tino once, but he also lived an ocean away. We had immigrated to Canada and all the extended family was still in Germany. My parents were frugal, though, and were able to save enough for us to visit Germany four times during my childhood. This was when flying was still a big deal and people dressed up for the occasion. It was between two of the visits that my dog obsession hit its peak. During this time, I received a dog guide of my own for my birthday. It was a small, white hardcover book that began with "Affenpinscher" and ended with "Yorkshire terrier," but I liked to imagine that it ended with "Zwergpinscher," German for miniature pinscher, so that I could say that I had memorized all the dog breeds from "A" to "Z." As I said, I was an odd child.

Then the time finally came to visit Germany again. I crackled with excitement. Tino! I packed two months ahead of time, although in the manner of a small boy without any thought for the need for spare underwear or socks. My mother corrected this later. We had to make a connection in Montreal and as we sat waiting to board, the dreaded announcement came — there would be a delay, possibly a significant one. In a moment of unusual candour, the airline representative detailed that the inbound flight from Frankfurt had sprung a fuel leak over the Atlantic and had been forced to turn around. I was crestfallen. Logically, what did a few more hours mean when I had been waiting months, years even, to see "my dog" again? Logic, however, cuts little ice when you're both tired and wired, at 11 years old.

There was another announcement. Lufthansa, the German airline, had graciously agreed to divert its New York–to-Zurich flight to Montreal to pick up passengers headed to Frankfurt. The degree to which this would be inconceivable today tells you how long ago this was. The agent walked around the waiting area, giving out seating assignments on new handwritten boarding passes. He apologized to our family of four. There were no four seats together, not even three. What he had were a pair together in economy, another single in economy, and a single in first class. Would that be okay? Or did we want to wait for another flight? I immediately blurted out, "Can I have the first-class seat?" My father, ever logical, said this would be fine. My brother Daniel was too small to be on his own, so he would sit with my mother, and my father was content to be by himself in economy. He had no need for luxury, and in some ways even found it offensive. That left me.

Within an hour I was in a world I hadn't even imagined existed. We never went to the movies in those days, and I only watched children's television, so "first class" and "luxury" were wholly abstract concepts. Flying in economy class seemed pretty darned luxurious to me already, so what proceeded to unfold was nothing short of astonishing. To begin with, the stewardess was plainly delighted to have me in her section, probably because it was a welcome break from the usual hard-drinking businessmen. The seat was bigger and cushier than the nicest chair we had at home, and I was immediately served my choice of juice or soft drink. I ordered ginger ale, feeling quite sophisticated as

I did so. Once in the air, the food kept coming — caviar, oysters, olives . . . I was delighted but becoming alarmed because none of this looked appetizing yet.

The grey-haired gentleman sitting next to me noticed my discomfort and leaned over to whisper, "You know, if you ask, they'll bring you chocolate truffles. They come directly from Switzerland." He was dressed in a dark suit, and I remember his gold cufflinks and gold tie clip. He was soft-spoken and friendly, evidently also happy to have someone other than a stockbroker or corporate lawyer to talk to. Conversation quickly turned to dogs, and, in particular, Tino. I showed him my dog book so he could picture Tino properly. I didn't ask what he did for a living or where he lived, but I was most impressed when he opened his briefcase to find a photo of his grandchildren with their beagle, because the case was filled with stacks of high-denomination US dollars and Swiss francs in thick, perfect rectangles. I don't know why the perfect rectangular nature of these bundles sticks in my memory, but it does. He didn't seem to think anything was remarkable about it, nor did the stewardess who just then came by to offer me more chocolate truffles.

First class — gotta love it.

The other thing that sticks in my memory was his confidence that my grandparents would bring Tino to the airport to greet me. I didn't argue with him, but I knew that Tino wouldn't be there. Only I knew that he was my dog. My grandparents and aunts and uncles and cousins didn't know this. But I was confident, very confident, that Tino knew that I was his person.

ASSUMPTIONS

Mrs. Martin screamed.

I almost dropped Rufus.

"What have you done to my beautiful boy?"

Now that I have set the mood, let me back up and explain how things got to this unpleasant point. Everyone knows the old saying about what happens when you assume. Even if you don't know the specific saying I'm referring to, I'm sure you're aware that assumptions can be dangerous. Factual knowledge is much safer. Veterinarians, and other professionals, sometimes assume a client understands what we're saying, when in fact they don't. This is dangerous. This can lead to people screaming and cats almost being dropped. I like to think that I take sufficient care to avoid this. I never say "cardiomyopathy" without explaining that it means heart muscle disease, and I never say "anything-itis" without explaining that it means inflammation of whatever that anything is in English. However, sometimes I get tripped up on the English. For example, I long assumed that people knew the difference between stomach and abdomen. Neither are technical medical terms, but they turn out to be synonyms for some people. So, when I say, "I'm afraid he's bleeding into the abdomen," they reply, "But he's not pooping or vomiting blood." So, over time I've learned to expand the description: "I'm afraid he's bleeding into the abdomen, by which I mean into the space in his belly around the organs."

In Rufus's case, I assumed Mrs. Martin knew what I was describing. I was wrong.

She had brought him in because he was developing mats. He was a gorgeous middle-aged long-haired cat, and he was a deep orange, like a Viking's beard. Cats develop mats for a variety of reasons, including some medical issues that can reduce their interest in grooming themselves, but Rufus was in fine health. Sometimes mats stem from arthritis limiting a cat's flexibility, but that wasn't the case here either. Most commonly, however, the cause is either obesity or disinterest. The first applied to Rufus, and probably the second as well. He was certainly a hefty customer, and I also got the impression that he was past caring about his appearance. But I could have been wrong about that.

"But I brush him all the time!" Mrs. Martin said. She was an elderly pink-haired woman in a vivid green pantsuit, so she and carroty Rufus made a striking pair.

"That's great! He'd be even worse if you didn't, but it never helps as much as we would like, because he needs to get his own saliva into his fur to prevent matting. It acts like conditioner."

"Oh," she said, looking unconvinced.

"I can get the nurses to buzz out those mats with our clippers. It's quick and easy, but I should warn you that he'll look a little funny after. Kind of patchy."

"Could they groom him too?"

"No, they're not groomers, but they could give him a lion cut. Would you like that?"

There. Did you catch it? If not, hang on. The punch-line's coming.

She paused for the briefest moment before answering, "Yes. Yes, please. That would be nice."

"Lion cut." Two simple English words that bring a vivid picture to my mind. Do they bring one to your mind too? And, far more to the point, are they the same picture? In my mind I have an image of a regal male African lion. The adult Simba from *The Lion King*, for example. See, he has a great wide mane of tousled fur, and a nice little tuft at the end of his tail. The rest of him is smooth. And that's what Rufus looked like. The techs left him a beautiful big mane and a cute tail tuft but shaved the rest down to a very short, sleek coat. I thought he looked absurd, but that's what a lion cut is, and it is inexplicably popular.

Unfortunately, it turned out that Mrs. Martin also thought it looked absurd. That's why she screamed. She thought it was not only absurd, but insulting to Rufus's dignity. And there was another problem — Rufus went outdoors in all weather. One can only assume (there's that word again) that Rufus was going to feel ridiculous and ashamed, but it seemed a safe bet that he was also going to be cold.

I stammered an incoherent apology. Normally, if a mistake is made, I do everything possible to make it right. I wouldn't charge for the grooming, but, as the old groomer's saying goes, "You can always cut more fur off, but you can't glue it back on." Actually, I don't think that's an official old groomer's saying, but it should be. Err on the side of doing less.

We were at an impasse. Mrs. Martin was livid. Rufus was disgruntled. I was at a complete loss as to how I could mollify them.

I cycled through a few more apologies, and then I had an idea. It would address the cold at least. The effect on absurdity and dignity was less clear, but personally, I thought that Rufus looked quite fetching in his midnight-black cable-knit sweater, purchased for him from the local pet shop by his remorseful doctor.

THE BATTLE CRY OF THE
SIAMESE KITTEN

While it is true that the great majority of pets labelled as aggressive are actually just scared, I have my doubts about

Supercat. The screaming began the moment I entered the exam room. Mr. Charles was a tall, thin man with a bright smile and a firm handshake.

"Sorry about that, Doctor," he said, still smiling. "Supercat doesn't like strangers."

"Oh, that's okay. He's probably just nervous. It happens all the time here."

Supercat was a new patient, and I hadn't checked the file before entering the room, so I was surprised to see a small Siamese kitten glaring at me from inside his travel carrier. From the volume and intensity of the screeching I expected a much larger animal. He looked like he weighed under a kilo, or not quite two pounds.

"How old is he?"

"About eight weeks."

"He's beautiful!" He really was beautiful. He was a classic seal-point with dark brown ears, nose, feet, and tail-tip, offset by a cream-coloured body and extraordinary sapphire eyes. And he was mad — not scared, mad. A scared kitten will scream at you from the back of the carrier while cowering. Supercat lunged at the bars as I approached. He opened his mouth so wide when he screamed that his whole face seemed to consist only of mouth, his eyes squeezed shut to little slits.

"Should I get him out?" Mr. Charles asked.

"Sure, please. He'll probably be better once he doesn't feel cornered in there." I doubted this was true, but I felt it was my duty to be optimistic.

Mr. Charles gingerly opened the carrier's door while making quiet cooing noises. Supercat shrieked at him and tried to swat his hand.

"Ooh, he's really mad today!" He pulled his hand back.

"Here, let me try." I don't know why I said that. If Supercat was willing to attack the literal "hand that feeds," how did I honestly think he'd react to my hand? I suppose it was my cheerful I-got-this doctor persona betraying me again.

As I leaned forwards, Supercat put his ears back flat and stared at me with an intensity that signalled a level of hatred two steps beyond loathing. He was quiet in that moment, but I could sense his battle cry gathering strength within. Each of his tiny muscles was fully tensed. I did all the right things. I avoided direct eye contact, I moved ever so slowly, and I spoke in soft, soothing tones.

Supercat let out an ear-piercing caterwaul and leapt forwards, smacking my hand with a velocity that made his paws blur. It was like watching Rocky Balboa go after a punching bag with the video sped up ten times. I pulled my hand back as if I had touched a hot stove. He had his claws out. There were four parallel red lines on the back of my hand, each beginning to sport tiny red beads of blood.

"Wow, he's fast!" I said.

"He sure is. Are you okay?"

"Oh yeah, just a flesh wound." I chuckled, but it did sting, and I wasn't keen to repeat the experience.

This was quite a few years ago, before most carriers were designed to have their tops taken off easily, so that was not an option. Plan B was a "gravity-assisted" exit from the kennel. I explained this to Mr. Charles and then gradually began tilting up the back of the kennel.

Supercat yelled like he was being dumped into bubbling lava, but he did not emerge. I kept tilting it up until eventually the kennel was fully vertical, its door swinging open above the exam table.

Supercat had starfished himself across the entrance.

He. Was. Not. Coming. Out.

Mr. Charles and I looked at each other and shrugged.

"Okay, on to Plan C then!" I said.

Plan C was a tech (veterinary nurse) with extra-heavy-duty leather gloves. I went into the treatment area where four techs were working on various things and called out in a happy singsong voice, "Who likes gorgeous fluffy kittens?"

Four hands shot in the air.

"And who likes gorgeous fluffy kittens *who channel Satan*?"

Four hands dropped. But there was a reluctant volunteer. "How bad can it be?" she asked. I just grinned wickedly in response.

The gloves probably weighed more than the kitten, but they were effective. The kennel was large enough that the tech could reach her armoured hands in and corral all of Supercat's flailing limbs. Getting him out of the kennel was only the first battle, though. We did manage to weigh him, and I think I heard his heart on the stethoscope between amplified screams, but the rest of the exam was cursory at best. I was able to give him his vaccine, which he didn't seem to notice as he was too busy gnawing on the gloves like a beaver on a log. He even fought us going back *into* the kennel. It was clear he was after a decisive victory, not just an uneasy draw. At least he was now officially a patient in the system, so I could prescribe happy pills for his next visit.

For the record, the happy pills did not work. On his next visit Supercat was more like a drunk screaming and fighting, but definitely still screaming and fighting. Over the years we saw him as little as possible. Fortunately, he was a very healthy cat. The angriest ones usually are.

BD-LD

I've introduced some of you to several worrisome veterinary acronyms in my previous books. If you read them, you would have learned HBC (hit by car), ADR (ain't doin' right), DIC (disseminated intravascular coagulation, a.k.a. death is coming), and I once briefly touched on BD-LD. It stands for "big dog little dog." It deserves a story of its own.

BD-LD does not refer to big dogs and little dogs bounding through the meadows together in harmony, chasing butterflies. It refers to big dogs attacking little dogs, resulting in a characteristic cluster of injuries, hence the acronym.

"What happened to him? BD-LD?"

"Yup."

I've mostly seen this happen in off-leash dog parks. By the way, here's an interesting fact: I do not know of a single veterinarian who takes their own dog to an off-leash park. Even when they don't have a little dog. Ponder that one for a moment.

But the one that sticks out in my mind is little Chico. His BD-LD incident was a kind of hit and run. The Penners were walking Chico down a quiet side street when a large black dog darted out of his yard (make sure your gates are properly latched, people!) and attacked him. It happened in the blink of an eye. Before they could react, little Chico was in this dog's mouth, being shaken. The big dog meant to kill. The Penners fought the dog, struggling to get Chico out of his mouth. Mrs. Penner was bitten several times in the process. The attacker's owners were nowhere to be seen. There was no car in the driveway and the blinds were drawn. Chico was screaming, but the big dog was curiously silent, not snarling or growling, just intent on his assault.

They managed to pry Chico out of the other dog's mouth and then sprinted towards home, which was several blocks away, carrying him, soaking Mr. Penner's shirt in blood. Fortunately, someone driving by offered to take them to the clinic.

Chico was no longer screaming. He was limp and did not appear to be conscious.

Everyone loved Chico Penner. As best as we could determine, he was a pug, beagle, dachshund, Chihuahua cross, about the size of a large cat. He was also so ugly that he was beautiful. Do you know what I mean? He was mostly toothless — I think he had two left — so his tongue lolled out to the side all the time, he had a chronic eye condition that made him look cockeyed, he walked with a pronounced limp, and he was roughly shaped like a yam — kind of tubular with a bulgy bit towards the back end. But he was a lovely, gentle soul, and he had personality in spades. Some dogs just have a special charisma. Consequently, when we learned that Chico was just minutes away and was in serious trouble, there was a general cry of, "Oh no! Chico!"

The treatment area of a veterinary hospital is normally a chaotic-looking scene. To the uninitiated observer, it looks like Brownian motion, with a lot of people going back and forth with random-seeming trajectories and speeds, narrowly avoiding colliding with each other. As soon as an emergency comes in, this changes. Instantly everyone's direction and purpose reorients and aligns. Little is said as supplies and equipment are readied and the whole room reorganizes itself to a single purpose. Within a minute, we were ready for him.

Chico looked appalling. He was in shock, so that needed to be addressed first. To my relief, the techs were able to get an intravenous catheter into him in seconds, but he was still in a perilous state. His body temperature was low and his breathing erratic. On a quick look, it fortunately didn't seem that the bites had penetrated his chest, but I was worried that he was going to lose a lot of skin if he survived because a large area on his back had been torn loose. This is vividly referred to as a "degloving" injury, which is perhaps more apt when it applies to a paw, but you get the picture. All the while Mr. and Mrs. Penner sat in the waiting room, stunned, Mr. Penner covered in Chico's blood, Mrs. Penner in her own. She refused to go to the hospital until she knew whether Chico was going to make it or not. They were a middle-aged childless couple. Chico was their world.

I won't leave you in suspense or drag out the gory part of the story, and I'm not going to pepper you with vet ER babble — stat this, two millilitres that, blood pressure this, capillary refill time that. You just want to know what happened to Chico.

He survived, but his injuries were horrendous. He seemed likely to lose at least a quarter of his skin. This led to a tough conversation. Chico's situation presented us with three quite different options.

First, we could attempt skin grafting, for which he would need a referral to a specialist, possibly out of province. It would be extremely expensive and did not have a guaranteed outcome.

Second, we could close as much of the wound as possible and then allow the rest to heal over on its own. This would require a lot of work with constant bandage changes and wound management, and would take many months. It also did not have a guaranteed outcome. Some wounds just don't want to heal.

And third, we could decide to let him go. He was 11 years old, which, while not really that old, isn't young either, and he had other health challenges. This was a really serious injury without a quick or simple fix.

The Penners chose the second option. They couldn't afford the first, and they couldn't face the last. They knew that his care would take a couple of hours every day, but that wasn't a barrier for them at all. And so, Chico's journey to healing began. I performed a minor surgery to remove dead tissue and to close what I was able to, but the rest was up to them. Every day they would have to perform hydrotherapy, meaning irrigating the wound to clean it and stimulate new tissue growth, dry it, and apply a fresh dressing. He needed pain medication and antibiotics, and he needed weekly checkups to monitor his progress and make adjustments to his plan. Through it all Chico remained Chico, just happy to be with people.

I wouldn't have written this story if it didn't have a happy ending. Obviously, I'm willing to share stories with sad endings, as I've often done so in the past. But I don't think I could have written about this if Chico hadn't done well. It took a long time. Five months, I think. But eventually the open wound, with its perimeter of fresh new-grown pink skin, shrank, at first imperceptibly, then more noticeably.

A circle the size of a saucer, then a coaster, then a dime, then a pinhead, then poof, it was closed.

The Penners called Animal Services to report the incident. If this dog could attack other dogs on the street, it was possibly a danger to children as well. The owner was apologetic. She said that her dog had never done that before. Her son had accidentally left the gate open. It wouldn't happen again. She paid for some of Chico's medical expenses, but eventually stopped. Her phone was disconnected, and it looked like she had moved away.

The Penners thought that Chico might be nervous walking by there, so they avoided it for a while, but the first time they walked him past that house, he didn't seem to care. And the first time he met a similar-looking dog, he wasn't scared then either. That's just the kind of dog Chico was. All his scars were on the outside. On the inside, there was only joy.

BELIEVE!

I had just finished the annual checkup examination for Kate, a beautiful Rhodesian ridgeback cross, and was scrolling through her medical record to find her vaccination history.

"Hmm, it doesn't look like she's had any shots since she was a puppy. Does that sound right?" I turned from the screen to face Kate's owner, Ms. Bancroft, a short woman about my age with a remarkably large smile.

"That's right. I don't believe in vaccines," she said, still smiling.

"Don't believe?" I thought. "Like not believing in Santa Claus or the Tooth Fairy?"

If I had been feeling puckish, I would have been tempted to fling open the refrigerator's door with a showman's flourish and then in a booming voice say, "You don't believe in vaccines? But I can prove they exist!" I would sweep my arm towards the gleaming array of colour-coded vials, lined up like ranks of obedient soldiers. I would then pluck one of them out and hold it up so the light glinted off the glass. "Behold, it is a vaccine! The legend made real right before thine eyes! Believe!"

But that would be mean, and it would be disrespectful. I knew that Ms. Bancroft was not stupid. She just had the wrong information. Moreover, I knew that by saying she didn't believe in vaccines, she was using shorthand meaning that she didn't believe they were a good idea. It came out that she felt they weren't natural, or safe, or effective, or in tune with Kate's inner cosmic vibrational energy. (Okay, she didn't actually say that last bit.) Ms. Bancroft was perfectly aware that vaccines existed.

If you are like Ms. Bancroft, then this story is for you. For the rest of you, consider it a refresher or skip it. But if you are a vaccine skeptic, please don't skip it. In fact, I've instructed the publisher to embed a self-destruct mechanism that will cause the book to turn into dust right in your hands if you skip this story. (Note to the rest of you: This will sound like a plausible threat to people who don't believe in vaccines. Sorry, I'm being mean again. I can't help myself.)

Let me now address Ms. Bancroft's three objections.

The biggest myth about vaccines is that they are unnatural, when in fact they are among the most natural of medical interventions. We are not defending the animal's health with strange unpronounceable compounds that linger in their systems, but rather we are training the animal's own immune system to look after that defence by presenting them with perfectly natural viruses that have been rendered harmless. All the benefit and none of that unpleasantness associated with developing immunity by actually getting sick. Also, your immunity does you little good if getting sick kills you. The skeptic might pounce on the "rendered harmless" bit as an example of how unnatural vaccines are. We also do all sorts of things to our food and drink to render them harmless. To call that unnatural would be to apply a definition of natural that precludes everything we've done since emerging from caves. Be my guest.

Of course, I didn't babble all that at Ms. Bancroft. I just said that how we vaccinate to prevent disease is far more natural than what we do to treat it if it is not prevented.

The second concern, safety, is easy to deflect. Reams of statistics are available, but in my experience, vaccine skeptics are mistrustful of statistics, fearing perhaps that they have somehow been manipulated by the big pharmaceutical companies. Therefore, my approach is anecdotal. I told her that I have been in practice for 30 years and have administered an estimated 70,000 vaccines during that time. And that's a conservative estimate. Through all those vaccines I have never seen a single life-threatening reaction. Not one. Of course, they can happen, but they are truly that rare. Many animals are tired for a day or two, and a small number are a bit sicker for a bit longer, but that's it. Honestly. Driving your pet to the clinic was more dangerous. Feeding him that extra bit of wiener was more dangerous.

Ah, but what about the more long-term effects on the immune system or causing cancer, she countered. That's tougher to refute out of hand. I could have gone on about how there is no published evidence whatsoever to indicate that, but again I reached for an anecdote. Over those 30 years I have only seen the life expectancy and quality of life for pets increase. We must be doing something right.

Finally, efficacy. It's hard to know where to begin with this one. The evidence that they work, and that most of them work extremely well, is immense. On the one side, we have zero evidence to show that they don't work. Not one study. Not one paper. On the other side we have stacks of studies and papers that must reach to the clouds if you put one on top of the other. Here, the key illustrative anecdote is that I never see parvo in vaccinated dogs, only in the unvaccinated. It's unusual not to be vaccinated for parvo, so outbreaks are rare now, but they do still happen. When parvo virus first emerged in 1978, thousands and thousands of dogs died. Once a vaccine became available, the number of cases and deaths dropped dramatically.

She listened politely to my three anecdotes, smiled her big smile again and said, "That's interesting, Dr. Schott, thank you. But I still don't believe in vaccines."

Belief is a funny thing. Once acquired, it moves from being something external that we agree with, to something internal that has become integral to our sense of who we are. A child who loses their belief in Santa Claus feels changed as a person and often feels a little sad. Humans will do a lot to protect the beliefs they hold dear, no matter how much evidence there is to the contrary.

BOB

By this point I've written over 150 stories for these collections. Appropriately enough, the majority are about individual patients. There are also some about diseases more generally, about the profession, and probably a few too many about me. There are, however, none specifically about any of my colleagues, with the possible exception of the story called "Benji," but that was more about the lion than it was about Al.

My colleagues crop up occasionally as secondary char-
acters and are often not even given the dignity of a name.
This is not because they are not interesting — far from
it — rather it's because I don't feel I have the right to tell
their stories. Veterinarians are an extraordinary bunch
and, given the nature of the work, all of them have tales
to tell. All of them. And in many cases, much funnier and
more interesting ones than I have. The only thing that sets
me apart is that in my spare time I write rather than fish
or coach peewee hockey or feed the homeless or any of the
other more common and useful pastimes my colleagues
get up to.

I want to address this imbalance, though, and tell one
story specifically about a colleague. He passed away over
a decade ago, so he won't mind, and it's a nice story about
him, so his family won't mind either, should they happen
to read this.

Dr. Bob Brandt came to Birchwood in the mid-1990s,
after Dr. Al Clark retired. For the first few years he and a
pair of silent partners just owned the clinic while he continued to work elsewhere. Consequently, we all formed
our impressions of Bob based on his occasional incursions
as owner. The practice was going through a rough patch
financially, so Bob came across as dour and money-focused
on his visits. To put it bluntly, none of us liked him all that
much. Then he announced that he was coming to work at
Birchwood. Imagine our collective groans. We were going
to have to work with this starched bean-counter each and
every day?

Well, it turned out that he did not count beans and he was not starched. In fact, he had a lively sense of humour (albeit mostly dad jokes) and that, even more importantly, he did not take himself too seriously. Some bosses will talk about how we're all in it together, but Bob would, without any fuss or preamble, clean out a poopy kennel, pick up trash in the parking lot, or help out the receptionists by answering the phone (although, as an aside, I'll mention that that specifically was not always helpful as he would frequently transfer the luckless caller to the void). This made a strong positive impression, and that impression was cemented by the dumpster incident.

The dumpster incident was the turning point. Before, Bob was "them"; after, he was "us." It happened one summer afternoon the first year he was working at Birchwood. I had a very anxious German shepherd named Kronos in to have a lump examined. The owner couldn't handle him, and we barely could either. He wasn't truly aggressive, but just so freaked out that it was extraordinarily difficult to do anything with him without taking considerable risks. Until we got the muzzle on, there were risks to our eardrums as well. He not only snapped at us like a Hollywood shark, but somehow simultaneously managed to shriek like he was on fire. This was an alarming spin on the idea of talking and chewing gum at the same time. In retrospect, I should have just sedated him, but I only needed him to be still for four seconds so that I could get a sample from the lump. Literally just four seconds. It took 20 minutes and three staff members to get those four seconds. But we did it. Exhausted, all five of us panting (the dog, the three staff, and me), each of us was so done with this experience. I transferred the sample to a glass slide and set it on an exam table before going up front to chat with the client. I think the three staff members went to dark rooms to sit quietly for a few minutes.

I quickly got sucked into a series of appointments and didn't make it back to the treatment area for at least a couple of hours. When I returned, the glass slide was gone. There had been a shift change in the meantime, so nobody knew what had happened to it. I'm usually a pretty calm guy, but I'm not ashamed to say that my calm failed me at the moment and I might have said some unfortunate words very loudly. I couldn't even begin to imagine how I was going to explain this to Kronos's owner after I told him how challenging it was to get the sample, let alone imagine actually getting a second sample.

Bob happened to walk by just then. He asked what was going on and then volunteered to look for the slide as he had some spare time. Before I could explain that I had already checked everywhere I could think of, Bob began to root through the garbage bins scattered around the treatment area. Elbow deep, he fished out urine-soaked paper towel after bloody gauze sponge, humming as he did so. Then a staff member pointed out that the bins are usually emptied at the shift change. If the slide had been accidentally tossed out, it would likely now be in the dumpster by the back alley.

You can predict the rest of this story. But I'll tell it anyway because I owe it to Bob. Without a moment's hesitation, he went out to the back alley, opened the dumpster, and bent over double to lean into it, hauling out garbage bag after garbage bag. He was still humming. And he found the slide. It took half an hour, and he handled lord knows what-all to find it, but he did it.

The lump was benign, so this is an all's well that ends well story.

There's not much evidence of Bob left in the clinic. Enough vets and staff have come and gone in my time that I have learned that an individual rarely leaves more than a fragmentary trace that they once spent years there. I suppose that could be seen as a depressing observation, but I'm a glass-half-full person, and I smile at the little bit of evidence that does remain. That small lasting mark. To this day there's a blurry photo hanging over my desk of Bob leaning into that dumpster. I think he would be proud to be remembered for that act. He should be anyway.

BUDDY

Buddy looked sad and bedraggled, with his eyes down and his head bobbing. The young man who brought him in reported that he hadn't eaten in a couple days and that he had bad diarrhea. He also reported that Buddy just wasn't himself and had stopped singing. I suppose I should clarify that Buddy was a bird, although perhaps the singing made that obvious already. To be precise, he was a little green-and-yellow budgie.

"He's not perching anymore?" I asked because Buddy was on the floor of his cage.

"No, he hasn't since this started," the young man answered, tucking his phone into the pocket of his grey hoodie. I had pegged him as being a casual pet owner because he initially gave off an aura of indifference, but now he suddenly seemed serious and intent.

"How old is he?"

"Seven and a half. I guess that's pretty old."

"Yes, it is, but they can live to ten. What do you feed him?"

"Budgie mix. The expensive stuff from the pet store."

"Is that just seeds? Are there any pellets in the mix?"

"There's vitamins and fruits and stuff."

Then I noticed his scaly legs and feet. "How long have his legs looked like that?"

"A little while. I thought it was part of getting old."

I was developing a suspicion. The commonly sold bird seed mixes are junk food for birds, usually with too much fat and carbs and not enough protein. Also, even with the better mixes, most budgies will pick out their favourite seeds, throwing the balance off and missing a lot of the vitamins. In the wild they are forced to eat a range of different seeds, grasses, and fruits, depending on what's in season. Consequently, in captivity they need to be on pelleted rations to have a balanced diet. In Buddy's case I wondered whether a vitamin deficiency had developed.

"By no means am I a bird expert, but I think there may be something going on with his kidneys."

"His kidneys?" The young man looked concerned.

"Yes. Birds pee and poop out of the same place, so often what looks like diarrhea is actually excessive urine mixed with the feces. Look here," I pointed at a spot on the newspaper beside Buddy. "See how the paper is wet in a big ring around the white poop? That's urine, and there's way too much. A common cause, especially in an older budgie, is failing kidneys. With seed diets they sometimes develop nutritional deficiencies that can damage the kidneys and cause the scaliness on his legs."

"Failing? That sounds really bad." He was definitely concerned. I felt chagrined that I had misjudged him. He really did care.

"Like I said, I'm not a bird expert and we don't have the right equipment such as a proper incubator to keep small birds warm, so I'm going to have to refer you to someone who can help with a more serious problem like this."

"Oh, okay. But can you give him any medicine here? And can you trim his nails? I think they're starting to bug him."

True enough, the nails were beginning to curl around. Buddy had probably been less active for a while and wasn't wearing them down.

"Sure. Secondary infections are common, so I can give you some antibiotics for him. I can also give you some advice on feeding him and getting fluids into him until you can see the bird vet. And we can definitely do the nails. Those do look bad."

Anybody pick up on my mistake there? This was quite a few years ago and I still wince when I replay this conversation in my mind. But at the time I was pleased to be able to do anything to help. The reception staff probably should have screened this appointment and sent him straight to the bird vet, but it wasn't clear on the phone how sick Buddy was.

Although he didn't look like he had the energy to bite, I put an old square surgical drape over my hand to protect my fingers, reached into the cage, gently wrapped the drape and my palm around Buddy, and pulled him out of the cage. It was like picking up a warm cotton ball. He weighed no more than 30 grams (an ounce).

"I'll take him in the back and get my nurse to help me with the nails."

I stepped out of the room, flagged down Amy, one of the techs, and asked her to come into the x-ray room with Buddy and me. A few years prior I had learned the hard way that an escaped bird in the wide-open treatment area was far more difficult to catch than an escaped cat or dog. The x-ray room was the smallest enclosed room and the farthest from the noisy parts of the clinic. I handed Buddy to the tech and she handed me the nail trimmers she had brought along. Boy, those were crazy long nails. Budgie nails are easy, though, as they are soft and the quick — the part that bleeds — is easy to see. I snipped one little nail and then Buddy let out a soft squawk.

"Wow, that's the first sound I've heard him make," I remarked, smiling because the squawk had sounded a bit comical.

"Um, Philipp, he's gone limp . . ." Amy said in an urgent whisper. I had been focused on the feet, so I quickly looked up at his face. Buddy's head had lolled back, and his eyelid membranes flickered for the briefest second.

That was not a comical squawk.

He was dead.

"Oh my God!" Amy and I said simultaneously. I briefly considered CPR and then dismissed the notion for obvious reasons.

"Shit!" I closed my eyes and sucked my breath in sharply.

"What happened? Did I hold him too tight?" Amy looked stricken.

"No, I could see you were being very careful. It's my fault. They can be so fragile when they're sick. They can die if you breathe on them too hard. Damn it! It was a stupid mistake to offer to do the nails. I shouldn't have touched him. And I should have warned the guy this could happen."

Amy didn't say anything. She looked like she was going to cry.

"What am I going to tell him?" I groaned.

Amy shook her head. "I don't know."

I stared at the floor for a minute and took several deep breaths. There really was no other way to do this. I walked back to the exam room, opened the door, and sat down heavily on my stool. The young man looked up from his phone and put it away again.

"How did it go, Doc?"

"I have some really bad news for you. I'm so sorry, but Buddy didn't make it. I guess he was just too sick to handle any stress. He was gone in an instant. He didn't suffer at all. But I am so, so very sorry."

I always fear the shrieking and wailing that sometimes erupts in response to sudden bad news. More often it's just sadness, perhaps mixed with confusion, and occasionally it's a businesslike calm where you can tell that they are keeping it together for the moment but will lose it soon.

Buddy's owner did none of these. He smiled, shrugged, and said, "Oh well. He was kind of messy and noisy anyway."

I was wrong again. I watched as he chatted cheerfully with the receptionist while paying the bill. He waved and smiled at me as he left. I waved back and forced a smile too. I know that Buddy was doomed regardless of what I did, and his owner's reaction should have made me feel better, less guilty at least, but somehow it just made me feel worse.

BUT THE PETS DON'T CARE

As I write this, Manitoba is recording record COVID case numbers. But the pets don't care. To the south of me, the world's most powerful human is behaving like my son does when I take away his internet privileges. But the pets don't care. A quick glance at the news headlines reveals that global climate records continue to fall like wobbly ten-pins. But the pets don't care. And it's the greyest of grey November days, with bare tree branches rattling like dry bones in an icy wind. But the pets don't care. Okay, to be truthful, some pets would care if put outside in that, but my woolly dog doesn't care in the slightest.

This is one of the major reasons why people have pets. Yes, it's for companionship, or to amuse the kids, or to get you out walking, or simply because you can't imagine a home being a home without a pet in it. But it's also because it is therapeutic to engage with a living being that is so blithely oblivious to the human news cycle and the traumas our species inflicts on itself. They don't care because they don't know. And that is such a blessing. It allows them to sail along from day to day, treating every day like pretty much all the days that came before.

Take Orbit, my dog, for example. His mood is the same every day. Certainly, he has moments of anger tinged with fear (what foul fiend doth knocketh on my master's door), and moments of naked avarice (please, oh please please please, let that sausage roll off the counter), and many moments of dull boredom (sixth nap of the day, don't mind if I do), but his lifelong baseline is a kind of rarified happiness that humans can only aspire to. Alas, our busy brains sabotage us at every turn. Orbit does not have a busy brain. Orbit does not care about yesterday, or tomorrow, or the world, or really anything other than this moment and this place right in front of him. I try to learn from this. Mostly I fail, but I do try.

This phenomenon extends to the clinic, where the doctors and staff are feeling more and more anxious as the pandemic wears on and the restrictions ratchet upwards. Yet our patients are much as they have always been. To be sure, some are more nervous because their people are asked to wait in the parking lot, but there are still lots of wags and purrs and joyous acceptances of treats. We are a very privileged profession. Almost every other job is tainted by the pandemic in more significant ways, or is radically altered or even eliminated by it. But the core of what we do — treating dogs and cats and rabbits and tortoises and the rest of the ark — is unchanged.

The other day the chaos reached a crescendo. We were trying to maintain two separate cohorts within the clinic, each keeping two metres' distance from the other. This resulted in a lot of dancing, shuffling, and maneuvering as doctors sought out techs in their cohort to help with their patients. The phones rang non-stop because every client interaction now involved phoning to and from the parking lot. The receptionist raced back and forth, dodging doctors, techs, and patients, as they delivered medicine and food "curbside."

In the midst of all this I had a little kitten with me — an eight-week-old grey ball of poof named Emily. Often chaos terrifies kittens and they hunch up and hiss from inside their carriers, but Emily was unflappable, purring and head-butting as I performed my examination. Somewhere in the background I heard someone shout, "Four hundred and seventy new cases today!" They were livestreaming the daily provincial COVID press conference. I felt myself tense up. Then I looked at the kitten. Emily did not care. Emily accepted a couple treats and continued to purr, even purring through the vaccination. And I felt a tiny bit better.

Incidentally, Emily ended up being a boy, so everyone, the owners included, got a good chuckle that day too. They decided that as he was such a cool kitten, he probably didn't have any gender identity hang-ups, so they kept the name. Emily, the carefree boy COVID kitten.

CAT LADIES

Admit it, when you read this title, you automatically added an adjective. Starts with "C." Has five letters. The expression is so pervasive in the culture that it's a cliché. And moreover, it's unkind and unfair. We're not going to use the C-word* today. Instead, we'll call them Eccentric Cat Ladies. Incidentally, I've also run across a couple of Eccentric Cat Gentlemen in my career, but this story only features women.

This subject came to mind when the *Free Press* ran a feature last weekend on Bertha Rand, easily Winnipeg's most famous Eccentric Cat Lady ever. Although she died 40 years ago, there's scarcely a Winnipegger who doesn't know who she was. She is even one of three "notable examples" listed in the Wikipedia article on Cat Ladies. Curiously, Florence Nightingale is another one. Why was she so famous? She was not famous because of the astonishing number of cats in her house — in and of itself not all that unusual — but because she publicly defended the practice.

Bertha rescued strays because she could not stand to see them suffer. Winnipeg's climate is not cat-friendly for half the year. She intended to find them homes, but when word got around that she was in the amateur cat rescue business, people began dropping cats off at her place far faster than she could find homes for them. This was the middle of the last century when there weren't nearly the number of shelters we have today, and the ones that did exist automatically euthanized stray cats.

---

* By the way, while I cannot and should not use the C-word, I've noticed that some of these people use it themselves. This is much like me as a German being able to call myself, or a fellow German, a Kraut. But woe betide any outsider who tries it.

Her neighbours were displeased by this turn of events and petitioned city hall to shut down Bertha's informal shelter. The fight was public and prolonged, with alternating victories on both sides. To bolster her case, Bertha had her house and its many inhabitants inspected by my predecessor at Birchwood Animal Hospital, who declared all the cats to be in satisfactory condition. But under pressure from the neighbours, the city wrote a special bylaw outlawing Bertha's operation. The battle raged for several years, with the bylaw even being overturned by a judge, but ultimately Bertha lost.

The story has an even sadder ending than you might imagine if you're not already familiar with it. She was limited to keeping three cats, but people just kept dumping them at her place, so the numbers grew again. Various crises ensued. Eventually she developed dementia and the state of the house and the cats began to spiral downwards. By the time of her death in 1981 her house had sadly become the worst nightmare of an Eccentric Cat Lady's house. It had to be torn down.

I've met many Eccentric Cat Ladies over the years, and while they are a diverse bunch, there are a few features that unite them.

First, they are driven by a level of compassion that is foreign to most people. The amount of time, energy, and money they put into the care of their charges is extraordinary. The need in most cities is essentially infinite. There are never enough shelters or Eccentric Cat Ladies to keep up with the multiplication of cats. Consequently, with that level of compassion, cat rescuing can snowball, as it did for Bertha Rand. "I've already got x number of cats, so what's $x+1$?" is a statement I've heard repeatedly. It's a bit like the parable of the frog not realizing it's being boiled alive because the temperature is increasing very slowly. These people are being boiled alive in kittens, which, I grant you, is a pretty weird mental image.

Second, they seem impervious to the opinions of others. Most of us will amend our behaviours based on rational argument, or a sense of shame, or universal criticism, or the law, but the Eccentric Cat Ladies do not. Their compassion is wedded to a sense of righteousness. In their minds, their cause is moral and just, and they are not afraid of a little ostracism and gentle civil disobedience.

Third, they are, well, eccentric. You can be brimful with compassion and fully stoked to fight the good fight, but it takes a special kind of person to put up with the comprehensive lifestyle adjustments required to live with dozens of cats. Eccentricity is defined in opposition to societal norms. Perhaps there is a parallel smelly universe somewhere where the norms are reversed, in which case having three or fewer cats would be considered eccentric (or, if you're a real kook, no cats at all), but that is not the universe we live in. I think it is possible to be eccentric and not mentally ill. In fact, I hope so, because I have my own eccentricities (please ask me about my map collection) and fancy myself to be completely sane. But mental illness does play a role in this story. It's obvious that some

Eccentric Cat Ladies are pathological hoarders. Others are delusional, and still others may suffer from attachment disorders. But in my experience, all of this is less common than the casual outside observer tends to assume.

Let me be clear: I am not condoning keeping large numbers of animals in your house, especially cats. I say "especially cats" because they are not herd animals, and many suffer stress in the proximity of more than a few others. A very general rule of thumb is one cat per bedroom. This is not to say that each cat should be assigned its own personal bedroom to live in, but when you are assessing home size versus cat capacity, this ratio can be a helpful guideline. However, as illustrated by Bertha Rand's story, sometimes the perfect is the enemy of the good enough. If all the shelters are full, and the alternative is freezing to death outdoors, adding a cat to your clean home and well-cared-for cat herd can be the lesser of a range of evils. Take careful note of "clean home" and "well-cared-for cat herd." These are the two elements that separate the Eccentric Cat Ladies who should be left alone from the ones who would benefit from an intervention.

And sometimes, as in Bertha's case, they can gradually slide from the former state to the latter. One of my clients appears to be going through this transition. Always spotlessly clean before, she now smells of cat pee and frequently looks dishevelled. I have literally lost count of the number of cats she's brought to see me. She's still sweet, seems sharp, and is reasonable to deal with, but I'm starting to fret about whether I have a responsibility to take action and call someone. I fear the domino effect such a call might set off. There are no easy answers.

CAT WARS

I'm not going to tell you a specific story. Instead, I want you to view this as a kind of fireside chat. Picture me in my armchair beside the fire. My three cats are arrayed around the room, at safe distances from each other for reasons that will be made clear shortly, and I am holding a scotch in my left hand. My right hand is for gesturing, as I do a lot of that when I talk. The scotch, if you're curious, is a Talisker, although it could be a Laphroaig or Old Pulteney. I usually only drink scotch socially, but in this imagined scenario you're in the room, so it's social. I don't know what you're drinking. You can fill in that detail yourself.

Comfy? Okay, let's get started then. We'll toast the good health of my cats, and yours, if you have any, and then I'll begin talking about cat wars.

There are two kinds of cat wars. The first kind is indoors, amongst cats that live together and know each other well. Think of this as a civil war, although it also has character-istics of a cold war as there are rarely any physical injuries. The other kind is outdoors, amongst cats from different households, or strays. This is a hot war, with frequent injuries, although never fatalities.

Cats are different from dogs (or humans) in so many ways, and this is another one of them. Dogs will sometimes fight to kill, but cats never do. And the indoor civil wars hardly ever result in any injuries at all. We see some scratched faces, but that's about it. They may scream and wrestle and roll around on the carpet like they're fighting for their lives, but they seem to always know just exactly where to draw the line. It's like WWE wrestling, full of drama and pathos, but afterwards everyone just saunters off to go have a drink, like they'd just been bowling rather than engaging in mortal combat.

The outdoor wars are different, but even there, serious injuries are almost unknown. The classic cat fight injury is the bite abscess. Typically, the client comes in with their cat reporting that he's been off his food a couple days. Sometimes they'll have noticed a swelling, sometimes not. I'll find that he has a fever and then ask whether he goes outside and fights. If the answer is yes, the hunt is on for the abscess. The big ones are obvious, but the little ones can be tricky to find. And there is rarely an obvious skin wound. This is why cats develop abscesses so readily. Their opponent's fang is like a hypodermic needle, injecting bacteria under the skin. Unlike in dogs and humans, where a festering sore would develop instead, cat skin heals incredibly quickly, trapping those bacteria under the skin. They rapidly multiply and the body sends in white blood cells to fight them, thus producing pus. A pocket of pus under the skin is an abscess.

The treatment is gratifyingly simple. Lance the abscess, drain it, and put the patient on antibiotics. They feel better the instant the pressure is relieved. Occasionally this happens on its own at home, causing many a cat owner to phone us in a panic. It takes a bit of explaining to reassure them that the explosion of pus is actually a good thing.

Why are there cat wars? Why can't they just give peace a chance? The main reason is territory, and cats have a fluid, postmodern view of territory, so it's more complicated than just drawing lines on a map. As mentioned in the previous story, generally speaking, cats just don't like to have too many other cats around. With strange cats, the tolerance is set at zero. Depending on how brave they are, they will enforce this zero-strange-cat policy with screaming, chasing, or attempts at abscess-making. They may also pee on your bed out of sheer stress and anxiety. Or if they view the offending cat through a window, they may take out their frustration on you or other animals in the house. This is called redirected aggression and is quite common.

Indoor civil wars are more complicated. Cats can become wonderful friends for each other, but for darkly complex cat reasons that I don't pretend to understand, "frenemy" situations are also common, where they cuddle one minute and try to thrash the tar out of each other the next. And outright enemies can live in the same home too. Curiously, though, if the enemies are housemates, abscesses are exceedingly rare, as is blood of any kind. But the sound and fury, that's something to behold!

Take Lucy and Gabi, for example, and then, later, Lucy and Lillie. Lucy was a first cat child and, for a short time, the only cat child. Then we brought home Gabi, a tiny adorable black-and-white fluffball, and it was war. The First Cat War. At 1,750 square feet and with four bedrooms, our house should be big enough for two cats, but Lucy didn't see it that way. Every one of those 1,750 square feet was her square foot.

Then Orbit, our Sheltie puppy, happened.

At first, both cats were bewildered. Why did you allow this wildlife in the house? It's not a cat and it's not a human. It must be wildlife. Some sort of a squirrel-fox thingy. They hated him. And then they suddenly saw each other with new eyes. *(Cue swelling violins.)* The enemy of my enemy is my friend! In fact, I love the enemy of my enemy! The war ended, and so long as Orbit stayed out of the way (which he did — he was terrified of them), there was peace in the valley.

Then the Second Cat War broke out when we adopted Lillie, another tiny and adorable fluffball. She was also unacceptable to Lucy. Gabi was indifferent, and Orbit was nervous, but for Lucy it was hate at first sight. That war still goes on today.

What can we humans do to broker peace when cat war breaks out? Our tools are limited, I'm afraid. It's obvious to most people that cats pretty much do their own thing without reference to us. However, we can bolt our cat flaps shut. This may not be viable if a cat is already used to going outside as it will howl and pester until you relent. But as more and more people don't allow their cats out in the first place, outdoor cat wars have become less common. Cat fight abscesses used to be a weekly occurrence in my practice. Now months can go by between them.

Indoors is trickier, though. The best I can offer is harm reduction by encouraging you to keep separate feeding and litterbox areas to reduce the contact between the warring parties. You should also make sure that there are plenty of high perches available by clearing some of the tchotchkes off your windowsills and the tops of your bookcases. Cats like to go as high as they can to avoid trouble.

There's usually one cat warmonger at the centre of the conflict, a little hairy Genghis Khan, Caesar, or Napoleon. In our case it's Lucy. She's great with people — visitors love her — but she's hell with other pets. That's often the way. In the worst cases we can consider medicating the aggressor to take the edge off them. Some anti-anxiety meds can be effective for that. You should also try the feline facial pheromone diffusers (ask your vet) to get some of that "we're all one big loving family" scent going in your house. It didn't work for us, but some people swear by it.

We've considered getting another dog, but that could just as easily make things worse rather than better. So, for now, we're like the UN — well meaning, but largely ineffectual. We haven't eliminated war among humans, and we're unlikely to among cats, but that doesn't mean we should stop trying.

My scotch is finished now, and the fire is dying. I'd suggest another drink and another log, but I see Lucy eyeing Lillie, who has apparently crossed an invisible line. This invisible line moves every evening. I fear that it's about to become too loud to talk. Have a good night.

THE CAT WHO DREAMT TOO MUCH

One of the things I love most about this job is its ability to surprise. Even after 30 years, surprise is still an almost daily occurrence. And sometimes I learn something completely new with these surprises. Take the email from Mr. Mercado the other day regarding his cat Gary.

Mr. Mercado wrote that he and his wife were concerned that Gary was having nightmares because he would move so violently in his sleep. He had attached a video clip for me to see what he was talking about. I smiled indulgently as I waited for the clip to load. I was always amused by how many people were surprised to see their pets moving or breathing heavily during their dreams. People sometimes did the same, so why not animals? In fact, some scientists believe that even octopuses with their alien nervous systems dream because they change colours while asleep.

The video started playing. It showed Gary, a large brown tabby, lying on a cozy-looking crocheted blanket at the foot of a bed. He was twitching and then went into a squirrel-chasing motion with all four legs. So far, so boring. Then it happened. Suddenly Gary began to flail his legs as if he were being chased by a pack of snarling rottweilers. He arched his back and sprang from his blanket. It looked like he would smack into an armoire, but he somehow landed on the floor on his feet. He bolted for the bedroom door, his windmilling legs a comic-strip blur. And then he stopped. He looked around with what can only be described as a puzzled expression and then calmly began to groom himself.

I've seen all my pets dream, my dog more so than my cats, and I have had hundreds of people describe their pet's actions while apparently dreaming, but I had never seen or heard of anything like this.

Mr. Mercado wanted to know whether there was anything they could do. Perhaps a sleeping pill? His wife had stopped dreaming since she went on sleeping pills. I had no idea. There are no "sleeping pills" for pets as insomnia is one of the very few conditions that our pets do not share with us, aside from a few unfortunate dogs and cats with dementia. I would have to do a little research before answering.

Many of us subscribe to a service called the Veterinary Information Network, or VIN. I mentioned it in a previous book. It allows us to ask questions of specialists and to search previous questions and answers. In the early days I was occasionally the first person to ask a particular question. Now the database holds over 1.8 million questions, so almost anything I can think to ask has been asked before. And so it was with Gary, the cat who dreamt too much. There were several similar discussions and one, from a vet in Pennsylvania a couple of years ago, that was almost identical. The veterinary neurologist who replied called it "extreme dreaming." Apparently that's a thing. Who knew? It wasn't necessarily a nightmare as they are no more likely to lead to acting out a dream than dreaming about something more pleasant. Perhaps rather than being chased, Gary was doing the chasing? Perhaps the squirrel suddenly looked extra juicy and had sped up? Regardless, the neurologist wrote that extreme dreaming was likely a REM sleep disorder. She recommended trying a couple of the drugs we usually use for anxiety management, as those have sometimes helped, but she felt that most of the time the people and the cat would just have to learn to live with it.

This will be easier for Gary than for the Mercados as I doubt that pets remember most of their dreams. They are blessed with minds that focus almost entirely on the present moment. In his mind, Gary had simply found himself on the floor of the bedroom, near the door, with his fur in slight disarray. This clearly called for grooming, not for fear or excitement about what had just happened. Can you imagine if they did remember their dreams? As smart as some of them are, it would be a stretch to assume that they could distinguish real memories from dream memories. Heck, people have trouble with that sometimes. We would have a lot more crazy behaviour in our dogs and cats if they governed their actions in part on things that happened to them in their dreams.

Now I know some of you are putting your hands in the air (figuratively), wanting to interrupt to say that your pet is in fact crazy in a way that could be explained by confusion between dreams and reality. You might have a point. Perhaps that dog who barks at a blowing leaf is remembering that leaves sometimes magically turn into angry cats, and perhaps that cat who is staring at the corner of your room at two a.m. is waiting for the giant rainbow-coloured mice to emerge from the wall.

I talked to the Mercados about trying medications, but they were nervous about the side effects. In the end we agreed that we may as well assume that Gary was enjoying the pursuit of succulent dream squirrels and just happened to be an extreme athlete in that regard. What would you do if you had a choice between dreaming too much and dreaming too little? I know what I would choose.

THE CONEHEADS

The official symbol of veterinary medicine is the letter "V" superimposed on the Rod of Asclepius (you know, that snake twining around an upright stick). The unofficial symbol, however, is the Cone of Shame. Before I go on to

discuss the cone, I want to say a word about the official symbol. That word is "lame." It's a lame symbol because it's derivative of the human medical symbol, making veterinarians look like a junior league version. If anyone is going to use a symbol with snakes, it should be us, and they should have to superimpose an "H" on it. We actually handle snakes, whereas most modern physicians run away screaming from them. The symbol originated from an ancient Greek healing cult involving releasing snakes among the patients. Presumably, this frightened the patients into at least claiming that they were feeling better so they could leave. As that's no longer the standard of practice, I feel the physicians should get their own symbol now and then we can keep the plain rod and snake without the tacked-on "V." Failing that, we could politely ask the veterinary surgical specialists to allow us to use their centaur logo for the whole profession. Centaurs are cool.

End of digression. On to the coneheads. Officially known as Elizabethan collars, or e-collars for short, these lampshade-shaped items are as indispensable to the veterinarian as the stethoscope, the syringe, and the scalpel. It's one of the things that distinguishes us from our human medical counterparts, although I'm told that a local vasectomy surgeon keeps a large e-collar in his office as a joke. What a card. Humans can be told not to lick their wounds and incisions and, generally speaking, they won't. Dogs and cats on the other hand . . . Well, the point is obvious.

So why do they lick? And is it even a problem?

Second question first. I have had quite a few people declare that it is natural to lick a wound. Yes, it is. But it is also natural to poop indoors. And it is natural to die soon after our reproductive years. Natural behaviours work best in natural environments and when there are no better alternatives.

Dogs and cats lick for two main reasons. The first is to clean the area. If it's an accidental wound, initially this can be helpful. By all means, get those bits of bark out of the cut from that sharp branch you ran into. The problem is that they don't know when to stop. In the wild, a wound would keep getting dirty, so it made sense to keep cleaning it, but our pets eventually come into a (hopefully) clean home. At that point they're just introducing bacteria from their mouths. A version of the licking-is-natural myth holds that their oral bacteria are beneficial. People who say this have never looked inside the mouth of a middle-aged dog with dental disease (which is to say most middle-aged dogs). It's like peering through the fetid gates of microbial Hades. There's a reason why you are always prescribed antibiotics after a dog or cat bites you. I remember a colleague who didn't bother, and her hand turned black. True story. But I'm veering into digression again.

The other problem with the licking instinct is that they cannot differentiate between a dirty accidental wound and a clean surgical incision. I imagine dogs and cats waking up after an operation and thinking, "What the heck? Those people were all so friendly and nice and petting me and saying how good I was but then, bam, I had an instant nap and now I wake up and there's this cut on my belly! Did they drop something sharp on me? Didn't they even notice!? Losers. And it's got these bits of string stuck to it. Groan. Oh well, I know what to do. It's just like those bits of bark that were in that cut from the Evil Stick . . ."

The second reason dogs and cats lick is for comfort. It likely, albeit subconsciously, reminds them of when they were small and their mothers licked them. It's soothing to them the way thumb-sucking or hair-twiddling is for some people. This self-soothing can become addictive and tip into obsessive-compulsive behaviour. Anxious cats will lick their bellies until they're bald, and anxious dogs will lick their paws until they turn rust-coloured (by the way, that colour is due to a substance called porphyrin in the saliva reacting with the air). A note of caution — sometimes these behaviours are also due to itchiness from allergies, so don't assume your pet is developing an unhealthy obsession and just slap the Cone of Shame on him. That would be agonizing if there's a legitimate itch. And there are excellent medicines these days for allergies. Even for true excessive self-soothing and anxiety, a cone is not the best solution. The necessary behavioural therapy for these guys is well beyond the scope of this story (now that would be a digression!), so ask your veterinarian for advice on this, please.

But for wounds and incisions, cones are still the way to go. Theoretically bad-tasting sprays and ointments are possible alternatives, but many pets laugh at these. You've seen what they're willing to eat, right? Fortunately, however, the cones have come a long way. When I first started in practice, we only had the rigid opaque plastic ones. Dogs crashed into things and cleared coffee tables with them, and cats got stuck under couches and in cat doors. The modern ones are clear, to improve peripheral vision, and a little more flexible. They're still a nuisance, though. Even better for some pets are the floppy cloth ones (true "Elizabethan" collars that Shakespeare wouldn't be ashamed to be associated with) and inflatable doughnut-style ones. I say "for some pets" because these are more easily defeated by the agile, the determined, the Houdini-like. You may have to try a few different options and sizes and means of attachment before you hit on one that is a reasonable compromise between nuisance and effectiveness.

Maybe the best veterinary symbol would be to put an e-collar on the centaur. You could also put one on the Asclepius snake, but that would just be dumb as snakes can easily reach around any collar. But a centaur with a cone wouldn't be dumb. Not at all. Right?

DEEP THOUGHTS AFTER
DROPPING BLUEBELL OFF

Yesterday I took my elderly VW Beetle to the mechanic because the check engine light had begun to flash, which I am told is OMG in car language. I'm not really a car person, but the Beetle has been with us for 20 years and I will confess a degree of irrationally sentimental fondness. We brought our first child home from the hospital in him and took him on great road trips before he was relegated to the role of "second car." Somehow his annoyances — refusing to start at random times, blowing fuses, making weird noises — have stealthily been reinterpreted as charming quirks and evidence of character. He even has a name, Bluebell, although I rarely use it. Not very masculine, but then the assignment of gender is at best a dubious practice when it comes to cars. It was bestowed upon him by a friend after I called his gargantuan white SUV Moby Dick. And his Moby Dick is a she. Don't know why.

Ron, the mechanic, took down Bluebell's information and hinted that I might want to carefully weigh the pros and cons of fixing what they might find, given his age and presumed imminent demise. I reluctantly agreed that, yes, that made sense. As an aside I'll note that I was amused when Ron observed that Bluebell had a "millennial anti-theft device." He was referring to the five-speed stick-shift transmission. I signed the paperwork, surrendered the keys, and bundled up for the walk home. They had offered a courtesy shuttle, but it's only a 15-minute walk and it was a lovely winter day. On the walk I began to mull the similarities between Ron's job and mine. In fact, I have occasionally even been called a "pet mechanic," although I suspect Ron has never been called a "car vet." To be sure, the differences far outweigh those similarities, but indulge me for a moment.

Both of our jobs divide into two general categories: prevention of problems and treatment of problems. And that prevention further divides into advice for care given to owners to apply at home, and preventative maintenance performed in the shop/clinic. The problems treated also fall into parallel subcategories as both of us treat accidents as well as illnesses, some of which are age related, some lifestyle related, and some just random bad luck (there's even "congenital" on both sides!). The main difference is in the treatment, as Ron always uses "surgery," whereas for me and my patients surgery is usually a secondary option, or not an option at all.

It was the preventative maintenance aspect, though, that dominated my thoughts on the walk home. I felt guilty because I had not brought Bluebell to see Ron in over a year. He gets driven very little these days, so the mileage didn't come close to warranting an oil change, but I knew that he should be looked at regularly anyway and assessed for lurking or impending problems I couldn't see. Perhaps a timely maintenance visit would have detected whatever ultimately led to the flashing check engine light? Part of the reason I didn't was that this last year just went by so quickly and part of the reason, if I'm honest with myself, was that I was afraid of what they might find in such an old car. I didn't want to have to get rid of Bluebell, nor did I want to face the potential expense required to keep him. The classic ostrich strategy. Avoid looking at the problem and it will go away! Except it doesn't. Well, not often enough to make this a recommended approach.

The metaphor is clear, isn't it? When I got home, Orbit greeted me as he always does, with the kind of unalloyed joy only a dog or a human toddler can muster. After petting him and giving him a treat, I lifted his lips and inspected his teeth for the first time in possibly as much as a year. They were atrocious. The plaque had become tartar and some of the tartar had mineralized and become calculus. The gums adjacent to the teeth with calculus were inflamed. None of this was painful or immediately dangerous for him, but left unchecked it would become both painful and dangerous. Maintenance was due. Overdue, actually. I softly said, "I'm sorry, Orbit" and offered him another treat.

We all know the saying about how ounces of prevention translate into pounds of cure. We also all know that our pets age much more rapidly than humans. And furthermore, we all know that animals are adept at concealing the early signs of medical problems. Yet, despite knowing those three things, sometimes we let that preventative maintenance slide. Since many vaccine protocols no longer require annual vaccination, we have seen the number of annual checkups decline as some clients only see the value in the shots and not in the examination and consultation. This is a mistake. As my reader, you already know this, but please spread the word to the people who don't. There are dozens of subtle things a veterinarian determines while examining an animal. At the risk of sounding condescending, there is really no way you can determine these things yourself. Even with the help of Google. Even with the help of your niece who used to work in a pet food store. Perhaps we've made it look too easy? Regardless, I hope it's obvious that waiting until your dog's check engine light begins flashing is a terrible idea.

Bluebell just needed a new ignition coil and some sparkplugs, so it was not nearly as bad as it might have been. Ron recommended that we also consider replacing the timing belt and part of the muffler soon. This was going to be expensive, but not nearly as expensive as getting a new car, and, hey, it's Bluebell. The day is coming when we will have to say goodbye to him, but let's not rush it.

DISPATCHES FROM THE FLOOFER CAM

I knew things had changed when Ms. Tran told me that she spied on Floofer while she was at work. She had set up a nanny cam at home and trained it on Floofer's enclosure. She always kept the live feed open in the corner of her computer monitor. I don't know what she did for a living, but it was in an admirably tolerant workplace. I should explain that Floofer was a rabbit, a handsome mottled white-and-brown French lop.

I'll get to why she was spying on the unsuspecting rabbit in a moment, but first let me elaborate on what I meant when I wrote that "I knew things had changed."

For the first half of my career rabbits occupied what can best be described as the second tier of pets. Dogs and cats lorded over them from the first tier, while rabbits, guinea pigs, gerbils, hamsters, rats, and mice were all lumped together as "caged pets." At the time, you only learned about them in vet school if you took an elective rotation in fourth year. The assumption was that people didn't care about these caged pets as much as they did about dogs and cats. They were viewed as somewhat interchangeable, or even — gasp — disposable. Ferrets, in case you're curious, wavered between first and second tier. And birds, reptiles and other exotica were first tier for their enthusiasts and specially trained vets, and unclassifiable for everyone else.

But this has changed. I'm not sure why it's happened, but rabbits are full-patch members of the first tier now. I suspected that something was afoot when I began noticing more young couples and singles acquiring rabbits as their only pet. Previously rabbits had mostly been purchased for young children as a consolation prize when the parents didn't want to give in to the demands for a dog or a cat. But now people were actively choosing rabbits for themselves in preference to the other options. And when the bunny cam was deployed, I knew for certain that rabbits had arrived.

The bunny cam was only part of Ms. Tran's intensive interest in Floofer's well-being. Long emails from her were common as well, usually with high-resolution photos of feces attached. There was also periodic mention of a spreadsheet, although I never saw it.

The problem was that Floofer was not a great pooper. She spied on him because she was terrified he would suddenly develop diarrhea and die. While her level of fear was exaggerated, it did have a basis in fact. Diarrhea is mostly just a nuisance in other species, but it can be fatal in rabbits. This is because they are hindgut fermenters. That explains everything, doesn't it? Probably not, but I don't want to bore you with the details of bunny digestion, so let me summarize by saying that you should think of rabbits as little cows. Nature meant them to graze. Their system is chock full of healthy, happy bacteria waiting to break down grass. When these bacteria don't get enough grass, they become sad and die. Their demise allows unhealthy, angry bacteria to take over that cause diarrhea and can invade the bloodstream, at which point it's curtains for the hapless rabbit. This can happen quickly, but not so quickly that a livestream of their toileting will make a difference. Check the, er, output once a day and you'll be good.

Floofer, regrettably, did not like hay. When I wrote that rabbits were meant to graze, I didn't mean on your Kentucky bluegrass lawn, but rather on the more nutritious grasses used to make hay. In this part of the world, it's Timothy grass hay. Ms. Tran was his second owner and the first had been persuaded by the pet shop that all the bunny's needs would be met with the packaged mix they sold. This was a blend of pellets and garishly coloured little tidbits advertised as "vitamins." On the one hand, the manufacturers were smart because this stuff was addictive, but on the other (larger) hand, they were dumb because it was nutritionally inadequate. I see it all the time — Bugs is hooked on his bunny crack and eventually his digestion begins to waver. So it was with Floofer. Ms. Tran tried all the recommended techniques and tricks to convince him to eat more fresh hay instead, but Floofer was stubborn. Give me my bunny crack, lady, or I'll starve myself to death. Then you'll be sorry!

When his stools started to soften, we were forced to resort to assisted feeding with "Critical Care," a powdered hay product made into a slurry. Assisted feeding is a euphemism. It means putting the slurry in a syringe, pinning the rabbit down, and squirting it into his mouth while he thrashes like the devil. Floofer may have been tough and stubborn, but Ms. Tran was tougher and stubborner. As of this writing, Floofer has recovered from each of these brushes with digestive catastrophe and is doing well, and Ms. Tran still keeps the bunny cam live on her desktop.

For the record, my money is on guinea pigs being the next species to get promoted to the first tier. It might go without saying, but in my opinion all pets should be there. I will be excited to see the first reports from someone's gerbil cam. And a little disturbed. But mostly excited.

DISSECTION LESSONS

The first dead animal, besides insects and roadkill, that ever I recall seeing was a beautiful blond cocker spaniel. I was about seven or eight years old. It was in a dense bush that I had decided to explore partway between my house and school. Its eyes were missing. To this day the mental image is so vivid that I can recall the exact position of this unfortunate dog, lying on its right side, most of its torso hidden under a shrub. But the missing eyes — those bottomless black sockets — that's what I remember most clearly. I recoiled in horror, backed out of the bush, and ran home. I never spoke of what I had seen to anyone. To this day I feel ashamed that I didn't have the courage to look for a tag and try to find the owners. I imagined them putting up posters. I imagined their distress at not knowing. I didn't have a dog myself, but I thought I knew what it might feel like. But I couldn't do it. I couldn't do anything that would summon that mental picture back to the front of my mind.

I think my existential dread of dead things began with that cocker spaniel. Most children have a degree of horror regarding dead bodies and such, but so long as it isn't human and real, this horror is usually also tinged with excitement and a tingly pleasure. I tried to read a book of spooky stories, but I couldn't finish it. I tried to watch a mild horror movie, but I had to leave. Halloween was sufficiently festive and fake that it didn't present any serious problems for me, but I was terrified at the idea of seeing, let alone touching, dead things.

Then in grade five we had to dissect a frog. I knew this lesson was coming weeks in advance. Those weeks were agonizing. I felt like a condemned man counting down the days. I was a science nerd, but dissection was a whole separate category, cordoned off in my mind from the rest of science. I knew it was necessary, but I had no idea how I was going to be able to do it. Touch a dead frog and cut it open and take out its insides? The thought made me want to hide under my bed, or vomit, or both. I tried to fake an illness on the day of the dissection class, but my mother wasn't fooled. I walked to school that morning in a state of absolute terror. What are the classic responses to terror? Fight, flight, or freeze, right? The first two weren't options, although I did briefly wonder what would happen if I just kept walking right on past the school. All that was left was freeze, and that's what I did. My salvation was that I had a lab partner, and he did all the dissecting while I stared, mute. Fortunately, my partner was gung-ho to cut up the frog and didn't mind in the least. And then it was over. And by some odd twist of fate, I was not required to dissect anything again all the way through high school and university biology.

You know where this story is going, don't you? Somehow, I became a veterinarian. And you will have surmised that while I might have been able to dodge the dead in high school and pre–vet studies, there is no way I could get through veterinary school without touching a lot of dead things. You are correct. Veterinary school features a lot of dead things.

I was 21 years old at the start of first-year veterinary medicine and considerably more mature than when I was in fifth grade, but a phobia is a phobia. There are people my age who screech as if in mortal peril at the sight of a spider the size of a paperclip. I'm just saying. Phobias are not rational, and they are often only weakly diluted by maturity.

The anatomy lab was on the ground floor of the vet college, tucked in the southwest corner with big double doors flanked by the skeletons of a cow and a horse in large glass cases. Why the big double doors? Look up for the answer. A rail ran along the ceiling, through the doors, and into an enormous walk-in cooler on the right-hand side of the lab. This is how the cows and horses got there. We first-years were dissecting cats, though. It always makes sense to start small.

Smell is known to be deeply and intimately bound into memory. One whiff of your grandfather's favourite brand of cigar, and you are instantly transported to his study, decades earlier. One hint of the aroma of your mother's Christmas cookies and you are five years old again, looking up at her, asking to lick the batter off the spoon. And one molecule of formaldehyde enters your nose, and it's the fall of 1986 and I'm standing in a fiercely bright room with my white-coated classmates, looking at 18 dead cats laid out on a grid of three rows of six stainless steel tables. But back then it wasn't just one molecule of formaldehyde, but enough to sting my nostrils and cling to my clothing and skin for the rest of the day. And in that instant, the anticipatory terror of seeing and handling dead things evaporated.

At the time, I didn't know why, but all these years later I think I do. Normally the worst thing to do to a person with a phobia is to overwhelm them with it. A gradual approach is usually better. For example, you don't force someone with a fear of crowds to go to the mall on Saturday. Eighteen rigid cats reeking of formaldehyde is the mall on Saturday of dead things. Yet, I think precisely because it was so overwhelming it snapped something inside of me. The feeling tipped from horrifying to absurd. The group camaraderie, which had been notably absent in grade five, helped too. Maybe it wasn't a true phobia after all. Maybe it was just a silly mental box I had built for myself and maybe that box was flimsier than I knew.

So, thank you to those nameless cats. Thank you for teaching me where the pancreas is in relation to the duodenum and thank you for getting me over my existential dread of dead things.

DOES YOUR CAT SMOKE?

Ms. Trottier laughed. "Ha! No, I don't think so, but mind you, every now and then she sneaks out . . ."

I was showing her the x-ray of her cat's chest. Bellatrix was a beautiful, sleek little black cat who had started coughing recently. I only ask the cat smoking question if I know the client well. After one too many blank stares, I learned that it's a good idea to get a measure of a pet owner's sense of humour before starting to drop jokes into a serious medical discussion.

"Interesting." I chuckled. "But let's assume no for now. How about any of the humans in the house?"

"No, not for years."

"Do you use any air fresheners, scented sprays, or essential oils around the house? Really, any product you can smell?"

"No, I don't like that stuff."

"Good, because cats can be extremely sensitive. I think Bellatrix has asthma, and sometimes we can identify triggers, but it doesn't sound like there are any obvious ones for her."

"Asthma? Really? Just like people?"

I have never stopped being amazed at people's incredulity that animals get the same diseases as humans. Ms. Trottier was a smart, well-educated person. I think she was an accountant or something like that in finance, so I'm sure there were aspects of her field that seemed absurdly obvious to her, but that routinely flummoxed outsiders. Once you know something, it becomes difficult to imagine not knowing it. (Except some of the weird trivia I know, like the date of the Peace of Westphalia [1648]. I can imagine other people not knowing that.)

"Yes, it is. Just like in people, it's an allergic reaction in the airways causing them to constrict."

"You know, we're doing some basement renos and it's been dusty. Could that be it?"

"Absolutely!"

"Can you treat it?"

"It responds really well to steroids. Hopefully once the renos are done we can wean her back off them, although sometimes once they're sensitized the bar lowers and the asthma gets triggered by much smaller amounts of dust or whatever it is."

Another neat and tidy diagnosis. Cat is coughing. Cat has been exposed to dust. Cat's x-ray rules out other, nastier diseases. Veterinarian diagnoses asthma. Veterinarian prescribes steroids. Cat gets better. Owner is delighted. Cat is presumably delighted as well.

But I'm getting ahead of myself.

I had told Ms. Trottier that the steroids would work quickly, so she was to call if the cough persisted. She called two days later. Bellatrix was still coughing. It wasn't that frequent, but it was quite violent-sounding, and she was concerned. I told her to increase the dose and call in another two days.

The two days passed and there was still no change. I debated recommending a more advanced diagnostic procedure, which involves collecting a sample from the airways for analysis, but this is not easy or reliable. I also debated recommending an inhaler, which is of course what people with asthma use. The cat inhalers are cute little face masks that go under the brand name AeroKat. But in the end, we decided that as the weather was warming up, she would open all the windows in the house and see if that helped. (It was April — in Manitoba the temperature can rocket up and down by 20 or 30 degrees from one day to the next.)

The next day she phoned again, this time sounding very chipper. Bellatrix had brought up an enormous hairball right after we spoke and hadn't coughed since.

Oh.

A hairball cough and an asthma cough are indeed remarkably similar-looking and -sounding. In both cases the cat extends its neck forward and makes a violent gagging, retching noise. The opposite error is far more common. I can't count the number of cats who have come in with a history of "trying to bring up a hairball for weeks" who turn out to have asthma. But this was the first time I had labelled a hairball cat as asthmatic. At least there was no harm done, and Ms. Trottier was very understanding. She was just delighted that Bellatrix was better.

I know that some of you are reading this and thinking, "Yeesh, this is interesting and all, but I'm glad this clown's not my vet!" For those of you keeping count of how many medical errors I have confessed to in my stories over the years, I'm going to ask you to please not be alarmed. I'm a dab hand at self-criticism and even then, I don't think my number of mistakes is above average. It's just that stories of mishaps are much more entertaining than stories of successes. How many of you really enjoy people's vacation stories that only involve them being relaxed and happy? Sure, a few sentences, but a whole long story about how pretty the beach was, or how nice the waiter was, or how clean the hotel room was? Forget it! The best stories are of the bus breaking down in the desert, or the unidentifiable meat on a stick that made you sick, or the shakedown at the border, or the drunken idiots in the next room. Honestly, they are. We are a shallow species who revel in schadenfreude. But we shouldn't feel too bad about it. Cats are the same, I'm sure of it. But at least they don't smoke.

DOLITTLE DREAMS

What animal lover has not had Dolittle dreams? Dreams of being able to talk to the animals, and — here's the key point — have them answer in a way that you can understand.

I loved the Dr. Dolittle stories when I was young. I can recall the covers of the books clearly. Dolittle himself was a stout fellow with a round nose, a top hat, and a fancy coat. He was illustrated surrounded by his animal pals, a monkey, a duck, a pig, a dog, an owl, a parrot, and a mouse I think, as they embarked on various adventures. I loved the adventures — sailing around the world, starting a circus, going to the moon — but most of all I loved the salient fact that he could speak what the stories referred to as "the language of the animals." He is taught this by his parrot, which made perfect sense to me at the time. I was also untroubled by the fact that Dolittle was a human physician who decided to practise on animals instead, without getting the requisite specific education. I didn't have any pets then and consequently only had a vague notion of what a veterinarian was.

But talking to the animals — how cool would that be? Sometimes I still fantasize about it. Now that we are in COVID lockdown and the clients are mostly staying in the parking lot, I'm often alone in an exam room with the pet. If they are unruly or just wriggly, I'll have an assistant with me, but I can usually examine the calm and quiet ones on my own. A conversation then ensues.

Me: "So, how are you today?"

Dog (yes, only in my mind): "Not too bad. A little freaked out. But not too bad."

I notice he's panting and keeping his distance from me.

Me: "Freaked out, why? Because your person can't come in with you?"

Dog: "Yup, that, plus I remember the time with the rubber glove!"

Me: "Don't worry! We don't need to do that today. You haven't been scooting, have you?"

I check the notes from the client.

Dog: "No, thank goodness. But are you going to give me a treat, or what?"

Me: "You bet, right now!"

I take two liver treats from the jar, hand him one, scratch him behind the ears and then hand him the second one.

Dog: "I see you have a whole jar of them there. Don't be stingy. I'm going to sit nice for whatever weird things you need to do, and then I'll get the rest of the jar, right?"

Me: "In your dreams! More for sure, but if I gave you the jar, you'd barf all over the inside of Mom's Volvo on the way home."

Dog: "Your point being?"

Me: "Ha! We're going to start by looking at ears, eyes, and teeth. Is that okay?"

Dog: "Sure, whatever. Just no rubber glove and no locking me in a cage either, right? I'll howl like a deranged coyote if you do!"

I agree and crouch down to examine his head and neck

and then rise to get my stethoscope from where it's hanging above the counter.

Dog: "Treat time!"

Me: "Sure, okay. You're being good."

I get a liver treat and at the same time take the stethoscope off its hook.

Dog: "Whoa, dude, what the heck is that?"

Me: "Don't you remember? It's a stethoscope. I use it to listen to your heart and lungs."

Dog: "If you say so. I blanked out last year because of the rubber glove incident. It looks weird. We don't have anything like that at home and I never see them on walks."

I let him sniff the stethoscope.

Dog: "It smells weird too. I think it was used on cat last and then before that on an old pug or French bulldog. Maybe a Boston. A girl for sure. Kind of scared."

Me: "Wow, you're good. That's exactly right! A 12-year-old female pug. And yeah, she was nervous. More than you even — ha ha!"

Dog: "Of course I'm good. You'll tell my mom, right?"

Me: "I'll tell her that you were a good boy, not that you were able to figure out which patients I saw before based on the smells on the stethoscope! That would make her wonder about me . . ."

The rest of the exam proceeds peacefully as we fall into a companionable silence. Then it's time for his vaccinations. He only needs rabies this year. I get up again to prepare that.

Dog: "Treats!"

Me: "Yes, of course. And a rabies needle."

Dog: "Yeah, whatevs. My mom is always telling me to brave for the shots, but honestly, I don't care."

Me: "You guys are much tougher than us. Humans are wimps."

Dog: "You can say that again! My mom stubs her little toe, and you'd think someone had chopped her foot off with a rusty axe!"

Me: "Ha! But to be fair, what about you when you get your nails trimmed?"

Dog: "Don't talk to me about that."

I smile and hand him his treat and then slide the rabies needle under his skin. He doesn't so much as flinch, but I can tell he's brooding about the nail remark.

Me: "Okay, that's it! I'm going to do up the paperwork and a staff member will take you out to your mom. See you next year!"

Dog: "Not if I see you first!"

Another book that touches on communication with animals is *The Hitchhiker's Guide to the Galaxy*. It is a cautionary tale. Arthur Dent is initially delighted when he is given a "babel fish" to insert in his ear as it promises to instantaneously translate every language in the galaxy. This has all manner of practical uses, but what excites Arthur most is that he will finally find out what the birds have been saying.

Well, that turns out to be a lot of "This is my branch. Stay away from my branch. Where's your branch? Did I tell you this is my branch? This is my branch." And so on. It was far better to enjoy their song and imagine something more interesting being said. Arthur deeply regretted finding out the truth.

Our pets are presumably smarter than Adams's birds and would have something less banal to say, but do we really want to find out?

DOOBIE AND GATOR:
A TALE OF TWO BUSH DOGS

It did not sound promising. Mr. Carter told the receptionist that Doobie had only been to the vet once, and that was after he had been viciously kicked by a former friend, and Gator had never been to the vet at all, not even once. No vaccines, no deworming, certainly no spaying. They were bush dogs from what he called "his shack" somewhere northeast of Beausejour, and they hadn't been in the city before. He was sure they were going to be freaked out. Why he didn't pick a rural vet instead wasn't clear. He made the receptionist promise to warn me that it would be difficult, and that I might get bitten.

As this was still during the pandemic, I went out to the parking lot to meet Mr. Carter, get some history, and bring the dogs into the clinic. He was driving one of those jacked-up monster trucks that are designed to drive right over VW Beetles without discomfort to the occupants of the truck. It had an array of spotlights on the roof, a gun rack in the cab, and a snorkel protruding from the hood, presumably to allow it to ford raging rivers.

Mr. Carter was standing beside the truck. He was a man about my age with a beard so large that I thought I caught sight of a small owl nesting in it. I don't know much about fashion, but if I describe what he wore as Late 20th-Century Army Surplus, does that create a clear picture for you? He fiddled with his mask as I approached and then, apparently exasperated, tore it off and stuffed it into his pocket. Fortunately, his body odour was powerful enough to make social distancing easy. I'm just stating the facts here, but I will confess that I was busily judging him. Right-wing good old country boy who's never bothered taking his dogs to the vet and will probably euthanize if I find anything serious. And it's got to be serious if he's going to the trouble of coming now after all those years. Sigh. Aggressive dogs, ignorant owner. I hate these situations.

"Hey, Doc! Which one do you want first?" He jerked his thumb towards the extended cab of the truck, where I could see two black dog faces looking anxiously out at their master.

"Oh, it doesn't matter." I glanced at the chart. "How about Doobie first?"

"Sure thing, may as well get him out of the way." He

reached up to open the door. Neither dog had a collar, but he fished one out from behind the seat and put it on the larger of the two dogs before letting him leap down.

Doobie was a black Lab cross of some sort. I couldn't read his body language at first, but he didn't look especially freaked out. I let him sniff my hand. He was tense, but he wagged his tail slowly.

Mr. Carter let out a low whistle. "Whew, that's a relief. He attacks one in four people."

That struck me as a remarkably specific statistic. I raised an eyebrow.

"Don't know what it is, but he's always been that way. And if you've been drinking, then it's even odds he'll attack you. Hates it when people drink. Maybe it's because I used to party too much!" He laughed.

"Well, that's good," I said, for no particular reason. "What did you want me to look at today?"

"He's been licking his paws and I need to get his anal glands squeezed. He's scooting all the time."

This didn't square with my image of a fierce bush dog, but okay.

"But don't let him see any other dogs when you take him in," he went on. "He hates all other dogs except Gator. She's his mom. He's killed loads of small dogs. Cats too. Kills 'em on sight. Goes completely psycho when he sees one. So, keep him away from cats too."

Mental note made.

I nodded and brought Doobie into the clinic, very carefully opening the back door, and then calling ahead as we proceeded down the back hall, "I've got an aggressive dog here!"

This kept dogs and cats out of his direct path, but there were still several to be seen. With multiple vets working during the pandemic puppy craze, it was difficult to fully clear the treatment area that the back hall led into.

I kept looking at Doobie, trying to gauge his reaction, but he was calm, and even quite happy-looking. He sniffed as we went along, wagging his tail. It occurred to me that only having been in one once, he had no reason to be nervous at a vet clinic. Maybe instead it was an interesting and entertaining place for him? Kind of like Disneyland. Except at Disneyland, they don't look in your ears, and they definitely do not insert fingers in your anus. But, when we got to that point, even for this intrusion Doobie was calm. He stopped wagging his tail and a looked briefly concerned, but otherwise he just kept happily glancing around, taking it all in.

At one point during the examination somebody walked close by holding a cat before I could warn them, but no matter — City Doobie was apparently a different dog than Country Doobie. He looked up at the cat and kept wagging his tail.

I described all this to Mr. Carter when I brought Doobie back out. He was flummoxed. Couldn't imagine how my report could possibly be true, but he was relieved.

Then it was Gator's turn. She had terrible breath odour, so he was worried about her teeth. And she had a chronic cough that was getting worse. Then it was time for the warnings. Apparently, she was a hellraiser and as much of a dog killer as Doobie. That's how she got her name. Even when she was a puppy, she'd gator-roll the other puppies, trying to kill them. Also, no surprise, Gator was a savage predator of cats. Bane of the feline species.

But she wasn't — at least not in the clinic. She was just as sweet and even-tempered as her son.

Mr. Carter was delighted. It was potentially going to cost a lot of money to address Gator's issues, and it might require a few visits, but he was keen to get going on it right away. He had misjudged his dogs, assuming a vet visit would be a catastrophe. And I had misjudged him. The way he looked and the way he talked caused me to assume that he wasn't a good pet owner. It turns out that he was a better pet owner than many far more polished people I have met. He really loved his dogs and he looked after them as well as he was able. I should have known better. I had been taught this lesson several times before, but apparently I'm not done learning it yet.

DOUBLE PUPPIES

On March 20, 2020, the province of Manitoba declared a state of emergency in response to the global COVID-19 pandemic. People were required to stay at home as much as possible. All non-essential businesses were closed. Veterinary clinics were considered essential, but we were to restrict ourselves to providing urgent services. Nobody knew how long this would go on, or if we would be forced to close completely if things got worse. I obsessively followed news from northern Italy and New York City, where the pandemic was hitting hardest, for clues about what might happen. My partners had just taken on massive loans to buy out the previous, retired partners and wondered how they'd be able to make the payments, and I was watching my own retirement investments appear to evaporate in the stock market. I also knew that many staff members lived paycheque to paycheque. We were all very scared.

I called a staff meeting that day and gathered everyone in the treatment room, which is the largest room in the hospital, so we could spread out. Twenty of us stood there in a giant wobbly circle, wearing masks, looking anxious. I explained that we would have to lock the doors and accept urgent cases only. The clients would wait in the parking lot while we took their pets inside for examination and treatment. Currently booked vaccines, routine checkups, and elective surgeries would be postponed to some unidentified point in the future. Moreover, we would split into two completely non-contact teams so that if someone contracted COVID, they would not take the whole practice down. One team would work Monday to Wednesday and the other Thursday to Saturday. Choking back tears, I told them that even though that meant reduced hours, we would continue to pay everyone full time for as long as we could possibly afford it. There would be no layoffs unless the clinic closed completely, even if it meant going into debt.

Then a strange thing happened. The phone wouldn't stop ringing. Almost everything even vaguely medical was deemed urgent by clients who were now, due to the lockdown, spending far more time with their pets. Even though we had cancelled or postponed all the truly non-urgent routine stuff, we only ended up being down a little over 20% in April. But everything took far longer now with the running back and forth to the parking lot and all the safety protocols, so the 20% fewer patients felt like double the amount of work. One important lesson during this strange time was how much clients normally help, just by holding their pets and keeping them calm. Now we had more nervous animals and not enough staff to help with every appointment. It was pandemonium. It was exhausting.

Meanwhile in the background larger forces were at work. As the lockdown eased in May, bike shops began reporting that they had completely sold out and were back-ordered for months or more. Contractors doing home renovations were booked for the entire year. Hot tubs were sold out everywhere and garden centres were booming like never before. And we just kept getting busier. Were veterinary clinics like bike shops, contractors, hot tub sellers, and garden centres? I dug deeper into the statistics and uncovered a startling number. I foreshadowed it in the title. We were seeing literally double the number of puppies compared to any previous spring. This is normally a very stable number that doesn't fluctuate much from year to year. But there we were in the middle of a global pandemic with double puppies. Kittens were up as well, but not by as much. And the trend continued through the summer and into the fall. We are now busier than we have ever been.

I asked around and, sure enough, other clinics were reporting the same thing. Also, the shelters were emptying out. Unheard of. What was going on here? At first the main theory was that people were at home so much more, so they thought that it was therefore an ideal time to train a puppy. As an aside, I'll mention that predictions were made that a generation of puppies would therefore develop separation anxiety when their owners, who had been home constantly, suddenly went back to work. As it happened a lot of people are still at home (I'm writing this in December 2021) and many others were able to make a more gradual transition, so I haven't seen much of an increase in separation anxiety. But back to why there were double puppies. Yes, the time to train angle played a role, but I think the deeper and more abiding reason has to do with the very definition of home.

Home is a place of love and comfort. When the world becomes frightening and unwelcoming, we withdraw into our homes and look for ways to fortify them. I don't mean this literally, although some people were apparently building ramparts of toilet paper. The fortifications we are building are of love and comfort. And pets are part of that. When many people picture the perfect, welcoming home, they picture a pet in it. Madison Avenue knows this. Hollywood knows this. I suspect you know this too. Dogs and cats are innocent to the mayhem beyond our doors and give us the same amount of love and comfort regardless of what the world gives us.

The pandemic is a terrible thing. Too many people are dying, too many lives are upended, and too many livelihoods are being destroyed. But even in this time, there is something positive to look at. In the words of Albus Dumbledore, "Happiness can be found, even in the darkest of times, if one only remembers to turn on the light." In our case, that light switch is marked "puppies and kittens."

DR. GOOD NEWS

I'm going to state the obvious: it's nice to be able to give good news. I've written before about how difficult it is to give bad news. How it doesn't get any easier with experience. How it breaks my heart every time. Given that I spend a lot of time performing diagnostic ultrasounds, I'm forced give a lot of bad news. Ultrasound is often recommended to hunt for terrible things like tumours or badly diseased major organs. Nobody says, "He's got a little rash. Let's do an ultrasound!"

There I go again, talking about giving bad news. This story is about giving good news, and that happens a lot too, even in the ultrasound room. In the early days I had a weird anxiety about not finding anything when I did an ultrasound. I was worried that people would feel they had wasted their money. Occasionally someone would express frustration that there was no diagnosis, but the great majority of clients were relieved, because they understood that we were ruling out bad things. Most beamed with delight. Some cried, they were so happy. Some even hugged me.

But the specific good news story I want to tell you does not involve ultrasound. It is about a lump on Digger's belly.

Digger was a small, shaggy mixed-breed dog. Mrs. Santos said that he was a spaniel-bichon cross, but I saw about a half-dozen other breeds in him. No matter, he was a great little dog and Mrs. Santos doted on him. He sported a variety of sweaters through the winter, despite having a thick coat, and he was often also adorned with seasonally themed ribbons.

"Doctor, I'm sorry, but I delayed coming because I was so worried about what you were going to say," Mrs. Santos said, clutching Digger on her lap. "I could barely sleep last night."

"I hope I can put your fears to rest. What's wrong with the poor boy?"

"I found a lump on him. It's on his belly. I hope it isn't cancer! I hope I didn't leave it too long!"

"Well, let's have a look. Let's get him up on the table, please!"

Digger stood placidly while I felt all along his belly. Mrs. Santos stroked his head and bit her lower lip while I did this. I couldn't find any lumps. This wasn't unusual. Clients frequently astonish me with the tiny things they find. Sometimes the client and I can spend ten minutes or so trying to locate a one-millimetre bump they noticed a few days prior. And sometimes we don't find it.

"I don't feel anything. Where was it exactly?"

"It's right in the middle. It's very large!"

"Okay, let's roll him on his side and then you can show me."

Digger was very compliant and happily flopped over. Mrs. Santos brushed his fur back and pointed at a pink fleshy object, roughly the size of a raisin, protruding from his abdominal skin.

It was a nipple.

I laughed, "Oh, I see! This is good news! It's only a nipple."

"But doctor, he's a boy." She looked stern as she delivered this news, apparently recalibrating my competence.

Um.

How would you have responded to this?

I briefly, very briefly, considered unbuttoning my shirt, but decided on a more tactful approach.

"Boys have nipples too. Many people are surprised to learn that." (White lie.) I smiled and patted Digger before going on, "This one is just a bit bigger than the others and has less fur around it, so it's more obvious. That's normal."

"Oh, thank you! I am so relieved!" She picked up Digger and hugged him. It looked like she was threatening to hug me as well in a kind of three-way that would squeeze Digger between us, but we resolved the awkward moment with an earnest handshake.

Faux tumours are my favourite kind of good news because the gulf between fear and reality is so wide. Nipples are the most amusing culprit, but ticks are more common. It's the start of tick season here in Manitoba, and any day now I expect someone to show up in a panic because this hideous tumour has just sprouted out of nowhere. It happens every year. Usually several times. To be fair, when ticks are engorged, you can't see their head or legs unless you look very carefully at the point of attachment to the skin. It is supremely satisfying to grasp one of these "tumours," yank, and pull it free with a flourish. I just feel bad for the client's embarrassment, but if there's any doubt, I'd rather they erred on having me confirm what we're dealing with, because the opposite has happened as well.

Faux ticks are not as common as faux tumours, but twice in my career, an abashed client has come in and asked me to check a small wound on their dog. They had pulled out a tick. Only it turned out not to be a tick. It was a wart. The fact that owner didn't also require wound management is a testament to the tolerance and stoicism of the average dog. Try to rip a wart off your spouse's arm and see how they react. But even this qualified as good news because the damage was very minor in both cases.

Our fears so often outpace reality. I love it when I can be Dr. Good News and allow reality to put fear in its place.

EMOTIONAL SLOT MACHINE

There are several nuggets of wisdom I try to impart to prospective veterinarians. I want them to understand that the profession is not an escape from people. It is quite the opposite, in fact. I want them to know that excellent grades will be needed to get into veterinary school, yet will become useless once they graduate. It's just a narrow fiery hoop that needs to be leapt through. And I want them to be prepared for the emotional slot machine of private practice.

"Don't you mean emotional roller coaster?" they'll ask.

"No, slot machine."

Roller coaster is the easy and automatic metaphor, a cliché really, but is it apt? Roller coasters go up and down and they are utterly predictable because you can see the layout (except so-called "dark" coasters, granted, but let's not get technical here). That is not at all what a day in the clinic feels like, or most of life for that matter. Moreover, all you feel on a roller coaster are cycles of anticipation followed by terror or euphoria. What kind of weird-ass coaster have you been on that makes you feel grief, or wonder, or anger, or depression, or love?

Slot machine is much better. There are two special modifications needed, though, to make this metaphor work. First, the cherries, bells, and hearts are replaced by emojis. Second, each pull of the lever is much more likely to bring up a row of the same emojis than a mix. If you feel that I am emotionally unevolved because I usually just feel sad, or delighted, or irritated, rather than multiple things at once, then feel free to imagine more of the complex blended emotions instead.

Got it? Now let's go through a typical day and see how this plays out. Yesterday was a perfect example.

First pull: sad faces. It was a euthanasia. Some hit me harder than others, and this was one of them. I had never met this woman or her dog before, but the fact that she was by herself, which is a little unusual because it's normally couples or families, and the fact that she was on the floor sobbing and hugging her dog, made it obvious that this was going to be a tough one. The dog's name was Misty, and it was clearly her time. She was a black 15-year-old shepherd mix who had lost the use of her hind legs. The woman kept apologizing for leaving it too long, despite my repeated assurances that Misty was numb in her hind legs, rather than in pain, and that there was rarely a perfect day for euthanasia, but rather a period of days or weeks where it is neither too soon nor too late. She was within that period. As I injected the euthanasia solution, she stroked Misty's head and bawled, "You're such a good dog. Mommy loves you!" over and over again, ever louder, as Misty's head sagged and her body went limp. The woman was practically screaming it when I told her that Misty was gone.

It was only through a tremendous force of will that my sad emojis didn't turn into a row of crying-my-eyes-out ones.

Second pull: laughing faces. I was running behind, so I had to go directly into a new puppy visit. I took a couple deep breaths to compose myself and then stepped into the room. A young couple beamed at me from their chairs, releasing a little brown fluffball who cannoned towards me. "It's your doctor, Benny!" they cried. Benny immediately pounced on my shoelaces and began tugging on them. The emotional shift was forced at first, but quickly became genuine. Benny was a delight, and he was hilarious.

Third pull: sad faces again. When Benny's visit was done, I stepped into the hall and saw Misty's owner talking to the staff at the front desk. She caught my eye and thanked me, stifling sobs. Oh God. Poor woman. The staff were asking if she wanted the number of a pet grief counselling service.

Fourth pull: serious faces. Next up was a phone call with a client who needed a detailed explanation of a dental estimate, and justification for why it was more expensive than the one their friend got for their cat at a rural clinic. None of the immediately preceding emotions were appropriate. It was time for patient, serious, and professional. I think they understood my explanation. I hope my tone helped.

Fifth pull: frustrated faces. A staff member was hovering, waiting for me to finish the phone call so that they could tell me that the roof was leaking again. Again! We have had the roof guys up there so many times! There's always a lot of "whaddaya gonna do" shrugging regarding old, flat roofs. It's patched and it's fine for a year and then it leaks again. So frustrating!

Sixth pull: relieved faces. I checked the schedule, and my next appointment was one of my favourite clients with one of my favourite patients for a routine visit. I was more than ready for one of those.

It's fun to look at my phone and see how many of the emojis apply to small animal practice. Besides the ones mentioned above, there's surprise, shame, fear, confusion, nausea, shock, skepticism, exhaustion, partying, hearts in eyes, stars in eyes, head exploding, goofiness, illness, nerdiness, devilishness and, of course, poo. Lots of poo. No cowboys, zombies, or clowns, though. Wait, actually, there was a clown once.

To be fair, three-quarters of the time we just pull regular smiley faces, which is moderately cheerful regular stuff with no lively emotional content. But it's important to know that several highly emotional, but completely different, pulls in a row are routine too. Consequently, I tell students that an ability to withstand this emotional slot machine is key to not burning out.

At least we rarely, very rarely, pull the bored face emojis.

ENCOUNTER IN THE WOODS

I like people. This is not a universal feeling in my profession. In fact, as mentioned at the beginning of the last story, some enter it thinking it will allow them to avoid people. Surprise! The animals come with people attached. But even though I like people, sometimes I want to be alone. This is impossible in the clinic and usually impossible at home too, so the best place to be alone is outdoors on a walk. Unfortunately, during the pandemic, aloneness on walks has become more challenging as 800,000 Winnipeggers, prevented from travelling elsewhere, shoehorn themselves into the available green space. Fortunately, we have a lot of green space and fortunately I have found some lesser-known trails, but the assurance of solitude that once existed is no longer there.

And so it was on a wintery Wednesday morning when I ventured down one of these secret paths through a beautiful aspen forest. This path and forest have a symmetry about them that I find especially appealing. I also love winding paths and mixed woods, but sometimes I'm in the mood for orderliness. This white snow-covered trail ran arrow-straight through a stand of black-specked white aspens identical in height. The straight, even lines in a black-and-white world were calming. I don't recall why I needed calming, but I did, and this was helping.

Then in the distance I saw them. Because the path was straight, I could see two people and their dog a long way away. They were headed towards me and as there were no branching paths in between, we were going to meet. This was fine. I wanted solitude, but encountering a few people here and there wasn't a problem. I just wanted to avoid the constant presence of people. Besides, they had a dog, and, as should be obvious by now, I like dogs.

As they approached, I could see that the people were an elderly couple, the man with a walking stick. Both were quite stooped and slow. I'm going to lie to you about the dog. It's a white lie, and a lie of omission. I know what breed he was, but it has nothing to do with what happened next and I don't want to feed breedist prejudice. So instead of naming the breed, I'll just say that he was a large dog.

The path was narrow, and the snow was deep on either side of the path, so it made sense for me to step aside to allow them to pass. They said good morning, and I smiled and said good morning back and took a big step to my right. The dog was on a long leash in the old man's left hand. I glanced at the dog as they passed and made the briefest eye contact with him.

In a fraction of a second, he lunged and snapped at me. Before I knew it, my left glove was off and in his mouth. Two my fingers buzzed from the padded impact of his teeth, but no skin was broken.

I was in shock. The old couple were in shock. The dog was snarling, hackles up, teeth bared, my glove still between his incisors.

Without any conscious decision having been made, I snatched at my glove and pulled it free. Then I quickly took several steps backwards, putting a couple of trees between me and the dog.

"I'm so sorry!" the woman said, while the husband strained ineffectually to pull the dog back. Normally the "I'm so sorry" is followed by "he never does that." I took note of the fact that they did not say that, and wondered whether they were on this lonely trail for a reason.

"Maybe he senses that I'm a vet," I said in an inane stab at lightening the mood.

They looked at me wide-eyed and didn't say anything further.

"You need to be careful with him," I added, inane again.

The couple both nodded, and after some more tugging on the dog's leash, they struggled farther down the path. I waited until the dog was well out of lunging range before resuming my walk, this time at a quick pace and with an eye to a route that had the lowest chance of encountering them again.

There's a perfect word in German (of course there is) for what I wrestled with afterwards: "Treppenwitz." It literally translates as "staircase joke." It refers to the clever retort you only think of after leaving a conversation. The rest of my walk was taken over by replays of the incident with all the things I should have said rather than the two ridiculous things I did say. But eventually I forgave myself and began to ponder the real lessons of that encounter.

First, I should not have made eye contact with that dog. I know better, much better. I would never look a strange dog in the eye in the clinic without first making at least a perfunctory judgment about his state of fear or aggression. Outside of the clinic these professional instincts sit a little looser in me.

Second, there needs to be more public education about which types of dogs are appropriate for which types of people. This dog was clearly "too much dog" for the old couple. Quite aside from any behavioural considerations, he was simply too strong for them. Perhaps he had been acquired for protection, or perhaps given to them for that purpose by one of their children. This is just speculation of course, but it is a scenario that I have seen far too often. It is never a good idea to get a dog for protection. The full reasons are beyond the scope of this story, but trust me when I say that it's true. If having a large well-behaved dog happens to make you feel safer, that's fine. Just don't get one with that intent in mind. A dog must be a companion who is safe around all people. Once you start drawing lines to delineate which people he can be safe around and which he can't, you're asking for trouble.

And thirdly, there also needs to be public education about the fact that all dogs benefit from thorough socialization and appropriate professional training. Too many people think they can just go on common sense, or what they remember from having dogs on the farm, or just hoping for the best. Often it seems easy, but I'm here to tell you that even the smartest people have trouble knowing what kind of training will actually be needed. A dog that learns to sit quickly and shake a paw is not necessarily a dog that won't bite. In fact, there is very little correlation between a dog's intelligence with tricks and their propensity to bite. Smart dogs who seem well behaved at home bite strangers too. Socialization has been so much more difficult through the pandemic, and some early statistics are showing an increase in bites. This dog looked young, and he might have been a pandemic puppy too. Consequently, even more attention needs to be paid to training and to those socialization opportunities that do still exist.

Biters aren't born, they're made. But that being said, very few people intend for their dogs to bite. It's a sin of omission rather than commission. They have omitted the act of research and proper training, not because they are bad people, but because they don't know. Maybe dog licensing needs to be more like driver's licensing, and the licence needs to be obtained before you get the dog and after you pass a test.

I felt bad for the old couple, because I'm sure they felt bad too, and I'm afraid they're in for some heartbreak down the road.

FELINE TRANSPORT LESSON

We're all in our bubbles. It's unavoidable. No matter how hard we try to cultivate empathy, we frequently have trouble understanding what it's really like to be someone else. Professionals have particularly thick bubbles. We are so caught up in doing our thing that we lose sight of how odd our thing is, as objectively seen by much of the population. The dentist pokes at teeth all day long, every day, and has a hard time keeping in mind that the recipient only has that done once or twice a year and is not nearly as comfortable with it. Ditto the lawyers and their verbose documents. Ditto the accountants and their obscure calculations. And ditto the veterinarians and their assumptions about transporting cats — among the myriad other things we assume, such as, "Just apply one drop to each eye." It's rarely a matter of "just."

My meandering point being, I don't think we veterinarians really appreciate how difficult it is to bring some cats to the clinic. Dogs are more easily fooled, only catching on once they get to the clinic door, but it is the rare cat who cheerfully saunters into their carrier, purring in euphoric anticipation of the double joy of a car ride *and* a veterinary visit! "Give up my sunny napping spot to be hauled off to a strange place where some random human will poke at me? Yes, please!" says that rare cat. On further consideration, I think that cat is so rare that you had better check that it's not actually a dog in deep disguise.

We blithely recommend exams and follow-ups and rechecks without giving much thought to how stressful this is for the cat and the owner. To be sure, most of these visits are medically necessary and unavoidable, but an acknowledgement on our part regarding the reality of the struggle is appropriate.

The cat transportation disconnect was brought home to me the other day when Lucy, our 14-year-old tortoiseshell, began vomiting more. We set the bar for concern regarding vomiting quite high. Many an evening we'll be sitting reading or watching television, and we'll hear that telltale hruk-hruk-hruk sound and just casually comment on it the way we might comment on the weather. "Wind's picking up again." "Cat's barfing again." The only difference with the latter is that we'll be mindful of where we step once we get up. But Lucy was clearing that bar. She was vomiting daily and, as we were slow on the uptake, she increasingly vomited right in front of us or, on one memorable occasion, on my lap. That got my attention. It was time to take her into the clinic for some tests.

But Lucy hates going to the clinic. Hates it, hates it, hates it. How much does she hate it on a scale of one to ten, where one is that legendary rare "Yes, please!" cat, and ten are the patients I never see because they have ESP and disappear specifically on vet appointment days? (By the way, there are lots of these psychic cats, and they merit a story of their own some time.) Lucy is an eight. She's ultimately a good cat who, while a fascist dictator with the other pets, is quite friendly with people. And she doesn't have psychic powers. But on pure loathing of the experience alone she rates that eight.

The standard advice is to disguise the transport kennel as a "happy place" by placing treats and toys in it. We've done that and I'm sure it works for cats at, say, five or less on the scale, but for the six-plus club, it just gives them more time to plan their resistance. Imagine someone's trying to force you to do something you don't want to do, like clean out the gutters or have an elective colonoscopy. Are you fooled if they wear a disguise and offer you chocolate bars? No. You're just more suspicious, aren't you? And a little weirded out.

Lucy took the treats and batted at the toys, but she knew the moment we switched from Happy Place mode to Clinic Transport mode. We still put treats and toys in, but she knew. Maybe she's a psychic kitty after all, or maybe she just picked up on our slightly more manic forced jollity.

"Lucy, look! Extra treats today! And that special catnip mouse! Don't you want to go in?"

Her facial expression was clear: "How dumb do you think I am?" She didn't go into the carrier. She just sat in front of it, regarding us with a wariness that told us that this was the crucial tipping point. Play our cards wrong, and she could bolt for the cat sanctuary above the basement ceiling tiles. The cats think of it as their secret rebel base. We know where it is, but we still can't get them out of there. We're like the Empire, with squeaky toys and bags of Temptations rather than the Death Star and Darth Vader. And even the Empire failed.

Move slowly and keep using the jolly treat-offering voice. Watch the escape routes. Be ready to pounce.

Lucy looked back and forth between us as we crept towards her. She was surrounded, but that didn't mean she was just going to surrender. Far from it.

I'm not proud of what ensued. Two veterinarians with a total of 60 years of experience between them trying to get their own normally quite passive cat into a carrier. And this is something we expect our clients to do all the time. We did finally manage it. Vets 1–Cat 0. But it wasn't easy. Even once we managed to stuff her in, Lucy was, despite her age, agile enough to keep hooking one paw after another on the edge. You'd pull one off, and another would shoot up. I swear she had grown extra legs. Octopussy. Eventually we sorted that out as well, and then the howling began.

It takes me ten minutes to drive to work. Einstein proved that time is relative. It travels at different speeds depending on a variety of factors. One factor he missed, but I'm sure future physicists will incorporate into their calculations, is cat wailing. A cat's wail slows time down. The clock on the dashboard still showed ten minutes (because clocks can't hear), but I know that 30 or 40 minutes of actual experienced time elapsed for both Lucy and me.

I was not angry at her. I was distraught for her. Lucy's cries were so heartrending that I felt like a terrible cat owner. What must she think of me?! Is there anything worse than feeling judged by your pets? Is there anything worse than fearing that they think you're abandoning them to a horrible fate? How do you people do it? How do you bring your animals to us day in and day out when this kind of stuff goes on?

I honestly felt like turning the car around and taking her home. I'm a veterinarian, for crying out loud. I should be able to figure this out without subjecting her to tests. This was utter balderdash, of course. Tests are essential sometimes and not having the courage to run them is a form of cruelty worse than a ten-minute (even if it feels like a 30- or 40-minute) car ride, and whatever stresses follow at the clinic.

I didn't turn around. And Lucy was fine at the clinic. She was scared, of course, but she was no longer caterwauling like she was being dragged off to hell by a brace of pit fiends. Her tests all came back fine. She was just constipated.

She yowled the whole way home too, but this time I didn't feel nearly as bad.

So, to you people out there whose cats hate coming to the vet, my hat's off to you. I get it. It is not easy, and it is not fun, but if you love them, it's what you have to do.

But explain "love hurts" to a cat, and see how far you get.

THE FIRST DAY

I wish I could give you the details. I wish I could tell you what the weather was like, or how busy the clinic was, or even what day of the week it was. I assume Monday, but that's not necessarily true. And I especially wish I could tell you about my first patient, my first ever patient as a licensed veterinarian. But I have no idea. It's not that I have a poor memory — in fact my memory is generally quite good — it's just that at the time it didn't seem like a big enough deal to be worthy of remembering. In retrospect, that's pretty weird, especially for someone like me who celebrates a raft of obscure milestones (I recently turned 666 months old), and who is so sentimental that he still has all of his childhood plush toys ("Woo-Woo" and the gang. Woo-Woo is a green corduroy dachshund. Shut up.).

This memory blank may be because starting at Birchwood just seemed like another small step in an ongoing series of small steps towards becoming a fully fledged, fully functioning adult. Moreover, I saw it as temporary. I'd work there a couple of years to save up to travel, and then after travelling I'd go to graduate school and eventually become a researcher or professor.

It may also be because I was clueless. A good example of this cluelessness occurred just a week prior, when I left home in Saskatoon, where I had continued to live all through university. On the day of that final departure, I packed my rusted-out old Honda Civic full to the point of blocking the rear window. It had all my favourite possessions (yes, including Woo-Woo), and even a few essentials. My parents hovered in the background. They didn't say much. There were hugs and kisses and goodbyes and promises to call when I arrived, but honestly, in retrospect I'm sure my mind was on which cassette tape I was going to play first. Given that it was the summer of 1990, it would have been down to Tom Petty's *Full Moon Fever* or a mixed tape of late '80s tunes sent to me by my friend Mark. The fact that this was a watershed moment in my life and in the lives of my parents was somehow entirely lost on me. Now that I have children of my own who are approaching their own de-nesting, my heart clenches when I think back on how oblivious I was then and what my parents must have been feeling.

Back to Birchwood. So, for all the reasons outlined above, I don't remember much about that day, but I do remember some things about the first few days. The first thing is embarrassing. It's how I dressed. I was determined not to be a doctor cliché, so instead I dressed like a different kind of cliché. I dressed like someone trying too hard to look casual, even though they don't feel casual. This meant polo shirts, cargo pants, and sandals. I'm German, so I wore socks in my sandals. This presented not only style issues, but also practical issues. It takes little imagination to come up with a list of reasons why sandals are a bad idea in a veterinary clinic. Apparently, I failed to conjure even that little imagination at that time. My bosses were tolerant folk and didn't say anything, but there were a few raised eyebrows. And on one especially hot day I wore shorts. Still more silent eyebrow raising. It took a fellow young veterinarian pointing out to me that my clothing choices were "bold" to change my perspective. When he said "bold," it was clear from his tone that he meant "dumb." Moreover, I looked like I was barely out of puberty and I was trying to command the respect of clients who were used to Dr. Clark, my tie-wearing senior boss who was a professional-looking veterinarian straight of central casting. He was so revered that a group of clients had given him a statue of a dignified veterinarian for his 25th anniversary in practice (my own 25th came and went with a clutch of Facebook likes). I decided that perhaps dressing the part would be helpful after all. And it was. By the end of the week, I had been to Eaton's and had splurged on three dress shirts, two pairs of nice pants and two natty ties. And you know what, wearing this, I weirdly felt more confident as a veterinarian. This is probably not weird to you, but it was to me at the time.

The other thing that I remember was finding out that Dr. Clark had been pressing his ear against the door of my exam room to listen in. I found this out because he told me. After a few days he sat me down and said that while he was generally impressed (the sandals were not mentioned), he had been listening to my appointments through the door and recommended that I describe the examination of the pet to the owner as I went through it. "Now I'm going to look in Fluffy's ears. What beautiful ears! Next we'll check out her eyes . . ." And so on. Apparently, I had been examining in silence. He explained that talking about each step was an essential part of the theatre of veterinary medicine. It added value for the client, and it helped to build a rapport. These were not things we had been taught in veterinary school, but okay.

After my first week of being a veterinarian I was professionally dressed, and I was talking people through their pets' examinations. It felt good. I eventually learned that I preferred to address the pet ("Now I'm going to look in your ears, Fluffy . . .") rather than the client, and I no longer wear a tie because of hygiene concerns (they're difficult to keep clean enough), but otherwise these two lessons from that first week stick with me today. When that quiet sandal-wearing new veterinary graduate comes into my clinic, I'll be ready for them!

A FISH STORY

One day last year during a break between appointments, I opened my computer to find a message from a colleague. Would I please call him to discuss an unusual ultrasound request? Cool. I pride myself on being willing to at least try any unusual ultrasound request.

"So, what have you got for me?" I asked, after the pleasantries had been exchanged.

"Promise you won't laugh!"

"I won't."

"It's a fish. A fish with a mass."

I laughed.

"Sorry, I know I promised," I said. "What kind of fish?"

"It's a fancy goldfish called a 'celestial eye' because their eyes are rotated upwards. He's got a mass on his side. I don't know whether it's a solid tumour, or a cyst that could be drained, or an internal organ protruding. I figured on the off chance you could ultrasound him, it would be a less invasive way of finding out."

"The owner must really love this little guy."

"He does, but it's also quite an expensive fish, and not so little. He's five inches long."

Oh. I had been picturing the classic tiny goldfish in the spherical bowl. You know, the kind that's single gulp-sized for a cat.

"I'm not sure how I would do that . . . I mean, how long can he be out of water? Seconds?"

"I had him out for ten seconds to palpate the mass. I guess that's not long enough for ultrasound?"

"No, unfortunately there's always a lot of adjusting and fiddling with dials until you get a clear image, by which point I'm sure he'd be in, um, distress!"

"Okay, makes sense. Thought it was worth asking, though!"

"Always worth asking. Sorry I couldn't help!"

After I hung up, I flipped through my ultrasound textbooks and had a quick look at some online resources to see if I could find a reference to ultrasounding fish. There was nothing. As I switched screens to start going through my other messages, a visual memory suddenly popped into my mind.

It was an image of a beluga whale, and she was nodding at me.

That's it! I picked up the phone.

"How does your client transport his fish?"

"In a big clear plastic bag, just like when you buy a fish from a pet shop. There's enough oxygen dissolved in there to last a little while."

"Perfect. He can stay in his bag and I'll scan through the side. The water will be my acoustic window."

The previous summer our family had vacationed in Churchill, which is in northern Manitoba, on the shores of Hudson Bay. Churchill is famous as the "Polar Bear Capital of the World," but it also hosts the world's largest gathering of beluga whales, in the estuary of the Churchill River. Thousands of the magnificent white sea mammals congregate there every summer, and we had the extraordinary privilege of snorkelling with them. The water was just barely above freezing, so this involved squeezing into heavy neoprene dry suits. Even so, the thinnest crescent of exposed skin between the hood and mask felt like it was being stabbed with ice daggers. But it was an inconsequential price to pay for one of the most extraordinary wildlife encounters of my life.

At first there was nothing to see in the murky green-glass water. It was like swimming inside a bottle of Heineken. Then we heard them. A flurry of pops and clicks. And suddenly they were there, swimming towards us: four sleek white whales the shape of chubby dolphins but the size of small sports cars. We were not allowed to approach them, but fortunately they were interested in us. One came face to face with me and began nodding. Delighted, I nodded back. Interspecies communication!

"No, she was scanning you," the guide said after I had flopped back onto the Zodiac like a wet sausage, babbling about what I had just experienced.

Oh. Never mind. But it was still super cool. "That big melon on her head is an acoustic lens. She knows more about your insides than your doctor does!" He was shouting now because he had gunned the outboard engine to take us back to shore.

This was the key to scanning the fancy goldfish. When I remembered the beluga scanning me, the solution to the fish ultrasound became obvious. Humans and animals are up to about 60% water in composition, and their average density is close to that of water, so ultrasound waves are tuned to most efficiently pass through water density. By using ultrasound, I was turning myself into a terrestrial beluga, albeit converting the sound waves into images that my far more visually oriented brain could process. I would scan right through the water in the bag to the goldfish. He would be moving in and out of the beam, but I could freeze the image at any point when he was in position. This would be good enough since I wasn't doing a detailed heart function study. (Ha ha! Goldfish echocardiography! Vet ultrasound joke. Never mind.)

The goldfish's owner was a very tall young man in stylish jeans, a white dress shirt and an eye-catching orange plaid sweater vest. The goldfish floated motionless in the centre of a large clear plastic bag on his lap. His eyes stuck out from the side of his head like two small marbles. Both were looking straight up at the ceiling and his owner's chin. There appeared to be no way to rotate them forwards. This must be an annoying way to live, I thought. I wanted to ask if he kept running into the side of the tank but thought better of it. Perhaps goldfish had some kind of special sense I should know about.

"Does he have a name?" I asked instead as I got the machine ready, having noted that the staff had just written "fish" on the file.

"Yes, his name is Bubbles!"

Of course it is.

I asked him to place the bag on the table while supporting it from the top. It was held shut with a chip-bag clip. I didn't want it rolling off and bursting like a water balloon on the floor.

I flicked the light off and placed my ultrasound probe against the side of the plastic bag. Nothing. Just black.

I couldn't see Bubbles. He must have moved away from the centre in the dark. I could widen the beam, but only at the cost of lower resolution, and when you're dealing with a creature only 12 centimetres long, you need all the resolution you can get. I could also pan back and forth, but if both Bubbles and I were moving it would be harder to get a good image, so I waited. Like a fisherman with his fish-finder sonar, I thought, although I don't fish and had no idea whether that comparison was accurate.

"Hmm, looks like Bubbles is hiding," I said.

Just then, before the young man could reply, I saw the fish move across the screen.

Wow, fish on ultrasound!

He was only on the screen for a couple of seconds, but I was able to scroll back through the clip frame by frame. I was entertained to identify various internal organs, and then there it was, the mass. It was fluid-filled, like a bubble — a bubble in Bubbles inside a bubble (meaning the bag. It's a stretch, I know). It appeared to arise from one of his kidneys, which lay directly under the body wall, causing the mass-like bulge. I had seen lots of cats with cystic kidney disease but had no idea whether that was something goldfish could have. In cats it's not necessarily serious, depending on how much kidney tissue the cyst replaces. Most of this kidney still looked intact, so I told the owner this was likely good news, but, as I wasn't a fish expert, his vet would give him more details.

It turned out this was a common goldfish condition and while it would eventually catch up with Bubbles as the cyst grew and new ones formed, it could take years to become a problem. Moreover, it didn't appear to cause any discomfort or unhappiness in the fish, so Bubbles could continue to patrol his tank, gazing at the ceiling, waiting to see his owner's beaming face.

THE HEART OF A LEOPARD

Every child has a favourite animal. In my case, there were several. I couldn't settle on just one, or rank them, lest it make the runners-up feel bad. How they would know about their rank, let alone understand or care, was not a question I thought to examine. My menagerie of favourites was almost entirely populated by the quirky and the odd: platypuses, kiwis, yaks, beavers, llamas, and the like. I'm not sure why this was. But there was one more traditional pick as well: the snow leopard. It wasn't because it was such a beautiful animal, as, given the foregoing list, looks obviously didn't register with me. Instead, it had something to do with its solitude and mysteriousness. The fact that it was so powerful but had almost never been seen in the wild made a big impression on me. This impression was cemented when as a teenager I read Peter Matthiessen's classic *The Snow Leopard*, in which the author goes to Nepal in search of the animal, but it behaves like a ghost, more a presence felt than something he could see. Cool.

Fast-forward ten years to my move to Winnipeg in 1990 and my first visit to the zoo. The Assiniboine Park Zoo had an astonishing collection of animals, including, you guessed it, snow leopards among its three varieties of extremely rare Asian leopards. These were not ghosts, but gorgeous flesh-and-blood creatures only metres away. There were two in the cage, draped over wooden platforms, lounging, swishing their magnificent tails back and forth, completely ignoring me as I gawped. By this point in my life I was much more impressed by beauty than I had been as a child. It was hard to imagine a more beautiful animal.

Fast-forward again, this time 30 years, to a phone call from the zoo vet. Could I possibly come to the zoo and perform an ultrasound on one of their snow leopard cubs? Normally they would bring the animal to me, but as the cub was small, they didn't want to have him away from his mother for very long. *Could I?* Are you kidding me? Could I ever! However, I kept my professional demeanour intact and asked her to wait a moment while I checked my calendar. Perfunctory checking done, I agreed. The cub had had some odd breathing episodes and there was a history of heart disease in his family, so they wanted to be absolutely sure he was okay.

On the appointed day we (my wife Lorraine, also a vet, came along as my assistant and was, if anything, even more excited than I was) drove up to a secure gate at the side of the zoo complex where we were met by the zoo vet and directed to follow her van. We took a winding route behind the enclosures until we came to the back of the snow leopard area. Lorraine was positively vibrating with excitement. I kept fending off paranoid thoughts that I had forgotten some important part of my ultrasound machine as I had never used it away from the clinic before.

We were ushered into a small wooden building and shown a metal exam table against one wall where I could set up my equipment. While I was fussing with the settings, I heard a gasp from Lorraine.

The snow leopard cub had arrived.

One of the zookeepers had carried him in from an adjacent building attached to their pen. She cradled him tightly in her arms, leather gauntlets protecting her hands.

He was stunning.

He stared at us unblinking with pale blue eyes. He was two months old and he weighed as much as an adult house cat, even though he appeared to be roughly double the size of one. Yes, that's how fluffy he was.

If the thought of a fluffy snow leopard cub that you can cradle in your arms doesn't already put you in a diabetic coma of cuteness, then consider the sounds he makes. This adorable bundle of fluff is a leopard, and he knows it. He knows that he is supposed to be a wild and fierce thing. So, he made wild and fierce sounds at us: "Grr! Grr! Grr!" Take it from me, nothing is as cute as something trying to be ferocious when it is manifestly not ferocious. At least not very ferocious. They did wear those heavy leather gloves, after all. The zookeeper said that they could continue to handle him like this without sedation until about six months of age.

The ultrasound itself was anticlimactic. In a good way. When ultrasound is exciting, it's because something is wrong. Nobody wants that. The room was darkened, the leopard growled quietly, and we watched a black-and-white image come flickering to life on my screen. It was the heart of a leopard, and its beat was strong.

HERE COME THE OLOGISTS!

I belong to a Facebook group for Canadian veterinarians. It's a marvellous resource for everything from getting tips on finding a washing machine that can withstand the rigours of hairy blanket after hairy blanket, to asking about experiences with new treatments, to just venting about the weird stresses we face that no Muggle understands. This morning there was a post from a veterinarian in southern Ontario asking what we all do when the local veterinary neurologist is unavailable on the weekend.

I guffawed, startling the cat, and almost snorted my coffee out my nose. "The local veterinary neurologist"? What local veterinary neurologist? I live in a city of 800,000 people, and the nearest veterinary neurologist is 800 kilometres (500 miles) west of here, at the veterinary college in

Saskatoon. There are precisely two veterinary neurologists in the 4,400-kilometre (2,750-mile) chunk of Canada that lies between Toronto and Vancouver. (The other one is in Calgary.) Consequently, there are hundreds of us for whom the answer to her question is, we do what we do on regular weekdays as well. I'll get to what that is in a moment, but first a word of caution.

The word of caution is that I might come across sounding like a crusty old practitioner with some of what is to follow, but I swear that I am not. Okay, I am little bit crusty. And I am old by some standards (but young by others!). And, of course, I am a practitioner. But when you string those three words together, it suggests an image of someone who is opposed to progress, who is an endless fount of irritating stories about the good old days, and who is just out of touch. That's not me. At least the first part isn't me — I'm all for progress. I'm just also worried about who gets left behind when it happens. Progress must be compassionate.

So, what do we neurologist-starved veterinarians do when a neuro case presents itself? We do our best. We remember our training, we crack the books, we talk to colleagues, and we check with neurologists online if we need to. I'm not claiming there's no place for a hands-on neurologist, but I am claiming that we run the risk of doing our patients a disservice if we are not willing to at least try without the help of a specialist. And we are doing our clients a disservice if we in any way make them feel guilty for not being able to afford a specialist when one does happen to be available.

It's not just neurologists: a whole slew of other olo-gists are playing an ever larger role in veterinary practice. Veterinary cardiologists, oncologists, gastroenterologists, urologists, endocrinologists, dermatologists, and ophthal-mologists are all routinely consulted now. And that's just a partial list. The last one, the ophthalmologists, have been around for a while as that is frequently a thin spot in vet-erinary education where general practitioners can rapidly find themselves out of their depth, but the others all repre-sent areas the great majority of vets felt happily competent in as recently as the early 2000s. Newer graduates (Crusty Old Practitioner Alert!), however, are increasingly trained to refer to a specialist as the default.

Again, this is not necessarily a bad thing. Veterinary medicine has become much more complex in the last 20 years, so the knowledge gap between specialists and gen-eral practitioners grows ever wider. It's great that these options now exist (albeit at a long drive for some of us), just so long as they are presented as that — as options rather than absolute necessities. There is a difference between saying, "It looks like Fido has injured his spine. Ideally, if you are able, he should see a neurologist" versus "It looks like Fido has injured his spine. He absolutely has to see a neurologist."

The arrival of the ologists is moving veterinary medi-cine closer to the human model, and it is driving up costs. For those who can afford it, this is not a problem, but there are still so many pet owners for whom a $5,000 procedure is just out of the question, and many others for whom it is a significant hardship. Consequently, it is so important that we continue to offer judgment-free choices. If we are not careful in this profession, we might end up allowing the perfect to become the enemy of the good enough.

Every pet deserves care. I have seen too many situations where pet owners have felt that euthanasia was the only alternative to pursuing a path they couldn't afford. Sometimes, sadly, it is that black and white, but sometimes there are other things that can be done, good-enough things.

I hope the colleague who posted to that Facebook group doesn't read this, recognize herself, and take offence. There may be aspects of her specific case that made a neurologist consult critical. It was just a convenient jumping-off point for me to present my view that people should be offered a Plan A, a Plan B, a Plan C, and however far down the alphabet we need to go until we find a plan that still has a reasonable chance of helping the patient, but also respects the client's needs.

And I hope that any ologists reading this take it in the spirit in which it was intended. I love you guys and I need you guys. I just don't want any pets to suffer or die because you weren't an option, and the vet didn't know what else to do.

HORSE AND COW AND PIG

I still routinely get asked whether I see farm animals too, or just pets. I get it. Most people's mental image of a veterinarian's patients includes the whole farmyard, in addition to the whole pet shop, and possibly the whole zoo as well. And people are just making conversation. It is, I suppose, the obvious first question to ask a veterinarian, even if the conversation is happening in the middle of a big city, which in my case it almost always is.

But no, as you the reader are already aware, I do not see farm animals. The gulf in knowledge and skills between pet medicine and farm animal medicine is very wide. They really are two different jobs. Consequently, there have been no barnyard stories in my three books, save an exploration of how to make a sheep sit in the previous one. No doubt some of you are disappointed. Short of making stuff up, there's nothing I can do about that except apologize and, as a consolation prize, offer you three brief anecdotes. All come from my time in vet school, which is the only time I dealt with these species on a professional level. Don't get your hopes up too high — they are just anecdotes, not truly stories.

The truth is I am afraid of horses. When I was about five years old, I fell off a horse in Germany. She was a slow, gentle dappled grey named Judy. A Super-8 movie exists of me gradually sliding sideways off her until I fall, head first onto the grass. Plop. To this day it remains unclear to me why nobody intervened. In the movie you can see my family standing around laughing. Comedy before safety, I suppose. Then early in my career I heard the story of a rural vet in Manitoba who got kicked in the head by a horse and died. Dead as a proverbial doornail. Yup, horses are scary. Funnily enough, Lorraine loves them and even owns one. In fact, I suspect that part of her initial attraction to me was my name, which is Greek for "horse lover." Ha ha ha. I should have been named Deiloshipp — "horse coward."

Anyway, the anecdote. It begins with three letters: PMU. Pony Magic University? You couldn't be more wrong. No, it stands for Pregnant Mare's Urine. In the 1940s smart people discovered that estrogen could be harvested from pregnant mare's urine. Through the '50s and '60s estrogen was increasingly prescribed to women after menopause. If you'll pardon the rude pun, a gold rush was on. PMU farms sprang up all over western Canada. By 1990 "Premarin" was the most prescribed drug in the USA. Since then, changing medical recommendations and the availability of alternative sources of estrogen, as well as controversy about the ethical aspects of the PMU industry, have reduced its market share to a fraction of its peak size, but this anecdote takes place in the mid-1980s, during the boom.

I worked several summers during vet school in an endocrinology (hormone studies) lab. One year, a few of us were sent to one of the largest PMU ranches in Canada to collect some samples for a research project. No, not urine samples — blood samples. The ranch was in the Birdtail Valley in western Manitoba, a good five-hour drive from Saskatoon. It was early May, and it was cool and rainy. We worked outside to collect the samples. These were half-wild horses. Sometimes the ranch used a helicopter to round them up. I was pleased by the rugged steel squeeze chutes which made being kicked in the head difficult, if not impossible. It was beautiful there and the work was easy, but it was cold that day. After a few hours, the researcher called me over and handed me a long rubber glove, long enough to go up to my shoulder.

"Here, Philipp, this will warm you up. I have a quiet mare here. Go ahead and palpate her and tell me what you feel."

He was right. I know this is going to sound gross, but it was wonderfully warm in there. I had inserted my right arm as far as it would go into her rectum. Happily, the horse didn't seem to mind. I suppose she was used to the bizarre habits of humans. I could have stood there all day, just alternating arms occasionally. Not only was it warm, but it was fascinating. The lower bowel was so mobile that I could move my arm and hand around her abdomen quite freely, palpating all sorts of things.

Hands-on anatomy. The goal was to find the ovaries and then determine whether there was bump called the *corpus luteum* that would indicate she had ovulated. I palpated while I warmed up and looked around at the green valley and all the horses.

I don't remember anymore whether I thought she had that bump and whether I was right, but I do remember an odd feeling coming over me: I liked horses after all. I was still nervous about them, but I liked them. Then the mare shifted, and I became mildly panicky and stepped away.

COW

Each anecdote will be shorter. The cow one takes place during our third-year Medical Exercises final exam. Medical Exercises was the class where you learned practical skills such as how to conduct an examination or collect a blood sample. Every student had to do it for every species. There were lots of guffaws about the future cow vets having to delicately open a kitten's mouth and about the future kitten vets having to lift a cow's tail only to get shat on. The class was actually kind of fun regardless of the species, but the exam was a practical one-on-one session with a clinician and could be relatively relaxed or absolutely terrifying depending on which clinician you were assigned. I was assigned Dr. Otto Radostits for my cow exam. Everyone laughed.

Every student who attended WCVM in Saskatoon from 1967 until his retirement in 2002 will remember

Dr. Radostits. He was one of those individuals for whom the expression "larger than life" was invented. He had a booming voice, an unblinking stare, and strong opinions. Mostly we knew him as the professor who had the dubious distinction of having made the most students cry. I was reasonably sure that I wasn't going to cry, but I was still extremely nervous. I was going to have to perform a full examination of a cow under Radostits's infamously withering gaze.

Thank goodness the cow was placid. I wasn't afraid of them the way I was of horses, but having a relaxed patient helped me relax. A little. The ace up my sleeve was that I was good at memorizing things, so I had memorized every detail of "the complete physical examination of the ox," as Radostits had put it during his classes. I took special note that he had emphasized the use of all the veterinarian's senses — well four of them anyway as I don't recall even Radostits expecting us to taste anything. He had a disdain for doctors who reached for tests too quickly. Almost everything can be determined by the complete physical examination of the ox, he claimed. So, I made a point of sniffing the cow's breath and palpating her udder, gently. Then I pinged her sides with my finger while listening with the stethoscope to hear if any of her stomachs were bloated and I described her gut sounds. I peered carefully at her skin and gazed in every accessible orifice. But most of all, and out of character for me, I took my time. Radostits remained quiet throughout, only nodding occasionally and jotting things down on his clipboard. When I was done, he shook my hand and asked me what my career plans were. I said research. He grunted and walked away.

In the end, the irony was that my best mark that year was in the complete physical examination of the ox. It was the last time I ever did so.

PIG

I don't recall ever examining a pig. Pigs just weren't brought to the vet college as patients. They were all kept in large swine barns and treated on site as a group, rather than as individuals. And during the weeks I was in the Field Services class where we visited farms, there were no calls to look at pigs. Consequently, my pig anecdote is from a lecture.

There were two ways to get the prerequisites needed to enter vet school. About half of us, including me, had gotten them through a biology program. The other half had come from an agriculture faculty. The biology students were required to take a class called Animal Science in first-year vet school, whereas the ag students could skip it. Lucky them. It was painful, so painful. Animal Science was a primer on the keeping of food animals with an emphasis on nutrition. I am not easily bored, but this was an exception. Flies fell asleep in that class. The instructor was undaunted, though, and gamely kept trying to perk our interest.

On the day in question, he made a remark that has become a beloved part of my basic repertoire of anecdotes.

We were discussing swine nutrition and he was pointing out how similar their nutritional needs are to ours.

"It's so similar that I always have to laugh when you students complain about how poor you are," he said. And then, raising his voice for emphasis: "It's an established scientific fact that a human can easily live off pig feed. So, if you guys are spending anything more on food in a day than 20 cents' worth of pig feed, you're doing so purely for your entertainment!"

I love that fact. I quote it often. Just ask my kids.

I apologize that this is not much of a pig anecdote, but at least you learned something that might be useful someday.

HOW TO GIVE A DOG A BATH

Before we dive into this (pun intended), let me ask you a question: Why do you want to give your dog a bath? I ask this question because most people err on the side of bathing their dogs too frequently. If you're doing so because you think you have to, think again. Puppy owners commonly ask me how often they should do it and seem genuinely shocked when my answer is "hardly ever."

Hardly ever is not never, so there are times when you should, but certainly not weekly, as some unnaturally

energetic people seem to be able to do, and for most dogs, not even monthly. There are so many "it depends" factors such as breed and environment and lifestyle, but on an extremely broad average, let's say a couple times a year, plus when nasty and stinky, plus in case of certain skin conditions. But never is fine too for lots of dogs.

Before I discuss those exceptions to the hardly ever rule, let me explain why I recommend bathing so infrequently.

And before I do that, a definition is in order. For the purposes of this discussion, I'm going to define bathing as involving some sort of soap or shampoo. If you need to hose off a muddy dog, go for it. And if your dog loves to jump in the lake, no problem (assuming he knows how to swim — Orbit swims like a bewildered-looking submarine). I'm not talking about getting wet. I'm talking about soaking the dog and lathering him up.

The problem with bathing is that it can strip the fur and skin of its natural oils and can disrupt the healthy microflora on the skin. The former can be partially addressed with the right shampoo, but the latter is difficult to avoid. Anything that cleans will clean off the bacteria. There was a time when this was thought to be a good thing as bacteria were all viewed with suspicion. Think of any cartoon of a bacterium — isn't it always an evil-looking little green monster? But now we know that the great majority of bacteria are beneficial, both inside us and on us. The same goes for our pets. Most people are familiar with the inside of us part through the explosion in the use of probiotics, but the on us part is only gradually coming into focus. Expect there to be a lot more discussions about over-bathing humans over the next few years, but once again, veterinary medicine is proud to be out ahead.

So, what about those exceptions? The nasty and stinky is obvious, I think. If your dog has rolled in a dead fish, or splashed around in a fetid marsh, or managed to coat himself with poo, please do give him a proper bath. As an aside, though, that sort of behaviour does beg an obvious question, doesn't it? Why would an animal who has 300 million smell receptors in their nose (compared to 6 million for humans), and who devotes 40 times as much of their brain space as we do to decoding those smells, choose to anoint itself in such powerful odours? Wouldn't it be overwhelming? Wouldn't it be like a human dressing in the most garish colours, and then rolling in glitter, and then wrapping himself in battery-powered Christmas lights? I have seven years of university education and 31 years of experience, and I still don't get it. Maybe they can't smell themselves? Some people seem to be that way.

The other major exception is a medical condition that requires bathing. This might go without saying but watch me say it anyway — here you need to talk to your veterinarian first. Please do not diagnose your dog with a skin condition and then pick up something from the pet shop. Retail pet shampoos are not regulated, and their claims cannot always be trusted. A discussion of skin disease is beyond the scope of this story but let me say one thing before moving on — people in general tend to be too concerned about dander in their pet's fur. If the dog isn't itchy, and the flakes aren't building up on the skin, then it's probably not an issue. But again, please check with your vet!

So, let's say one of the exceptions applies, or it's the couple times a year that I said it was okay to bathe your dog for purely aesthetic reasons so that he is all shiny and new-looking, how do you do it? That is, after all, the title of the story. The actual technique will vary with the size of the dog and with his willingness to participate. But regardless, be prepared to get wet. Unless your dog is tiny, or comatose, or you have exceptionally long arms, you will get wet, especially if you do it right. Doing it right means rinsing the shampoo off very thoroughly, during which your dog will likely want to shake. The first time that happens when he's a puppy it's kind of comical and cute, but I can attest that the novelty wears off very quickly.

There are a couple other important points regarding bathing. The first is to use a pet shampoo. This may seem obvious, but an amazing number of people still want to use human baby shampoo. Yes, it's gentle, but the pH balance is wrong. And with the pet shampoos, pick the simplest one. Do not use any overly scented ones and especially any that claim to treat anything. The second point is to avoid getting water in your dog's ears (or, obviously, eyes). Their ear canals are quite deep and are difficult to dry properly, so infections can result.

That's it. So, this wasn't really so much about "How to Give a Dog a Bath" as it was an effort to discourage you from doing so, or at least doing so too often, but I thought the title was a cute echo of the "How to Give a Cat a Pill" story from *The Accidental Veterinarian*. I will carry on that echo by saying that there will not be a "How to Give a Cat a Bath" story. Bathing cats requires more courage, strength, stamina, and foolhardiness than most of us can lay claim to, but thankfully, the cats manage it all very well by themselves. Nature has been kind to us in this regard at least.

THE INTERVIEWS

We interviewed a new veterinarian the other day, after which I reflected on my own checkered history with interviews. When I looked back on them, I realized that I never got any of the jobs I interviewed for. Not one. All the jobs I have had, including my current one, I stumbled into through various other avenues.

My first job was simply assigned to me. I put my name on the list at the "Odd Job Squad" in Saskatoon in the summer of 1983 and was told to go mow the lawn behind a local photography studio. This, I could do, but it was all downhill from there. The ensuing jobs were all wildly unsuited for a bookish teen with the build of a famine victim. Ripping bolted chairs out of a theatre, pouring cement, hefting debris . . . I lasted only a day in each one. The following summer I was again assigned a job, this time through the student job bank, and this time supervising convicts in a misguided and mismanaged organic vegetable growing project. Mayhem, fires, embezzlement, bingo, and prairie snorkelling ensued. But these are not stories for a veterinary-themed book, so I'll leave you to wonder.

The first job that I actively sought out and interviewed for was with the Canadian Wildlife Service. I was in pre-veterinary studies at the University of Saskatchewan, but still on the fence about whether I wanted to stick with that plan or keep working on my biology degree with the aim of becoming a wildlife biologist. My credits could be used either way. Those of you who have read *The Accidental Veterinarian* know that I only picked veterinary medicine because I had gone through the alphabetical university course calendar and had ruled out everything else by the time I arrived at "V," the last letter represented. Consequently, there was no particular fire in my belly, and although I could have applied after two years of pre-veterinary studies, I postponed my application for another year. Let's give wildlife biology a proper try first, I thought. I liked the idea of research.

The Canadian Wildlife Service hired its summer students through a system where you applied to the whole service and then individual researchers would pick through the pool of candidates and decide which ones they would like to interview for their projects. I was granted two interviews. This was pretty exciting because I worried that my resumé, featuring lawn mowing and failed large-scale vegetable gardening projects, would not excite any interest. I wondered whether perhaps they had called one of the biology professors I had listed as a reference, but I wasn't sure how far an accolade about me being a dab hand at multiple choice questions on mitosis would get me.

The first interview, really my first ever interview, was with a heavily bearded fellow in a cardigan with thick glasses that magnified his eyes slightly. He had an impressive office with floor-to-ceiling bookcases along all the walls. All I knew about him was that he was an ornithologist. We shook hands and then he asked me to sit down opposite him at his large desk. His desk was cluttered with papers and notebooks. Curiously, it also had a record player at one end.

Here we go, I thought. I had read up on the interview process and was ready with answers about reliability, punctuality, salary expectations, and ability to get along with others. The researcher, however, did not start by asking me any questions. He smiled, stood up, and walked to one of the bookcases. Pausing for a moment, he selected a record album.

Okay, a little music to set a relaxed tone. A bit irregular, I suppose, but as my father was a physics professor, I had the inside track on how odd these people could be.

Then I saw the album cover: *Bird Songs of Western Canada.*

Uh-oh.

"Let's see what you can identify," he said, sitting back down.

This was going to be awkward.

To this day I still marvel at how I spoke up right away, rather than trying to muddle through, which is my more usual reflex. "I'm sorry, sir, but if they're not all crow calls, I don't think I'll be able to identify any." This was the pathetic truth.

Crestfallen, he set the record down on his desk. "That's too bad. The project is to do bird counts at dawn by identifying the song. Distinguishing the different warbler species is particularly challenging."

We agreed that while I could try to learn the songs in advance, he had several more interviews to go through, including one student who was active in the local bird-watching community.

The second interview was just down the hall. This office had fewer bookcases, and more maps on the wall, as well as framed photographs from what looked like the Arctic. Bearded again, but Grateful Dead T-shirt rather than cardigan, and no glasses.

This interview was more traditional with a series of questions, but it was over almost as quickly.

First question: "Are you comfortable handling a rifle?"

Answer: "I've never even been in the same room as one."

Frown. Second question: "How are you with heights?"

Answer: "Well, I don't mind being up high if there's a railing or something, but I get pretty nervous if there's just a big drop in front of me."

Another frown. "I'm sorry, but I don't think this will work out then. The project involves climbing high cliffs on Baffin Island to count seabird eggs. The rifle is for the polar bears."

Ah.

Wildlife biology . . . cool in theory, but was I suited for the reality?

I ended up getting a job in a reproductive biology research lab through a fellow student who recommended me. No interview, no questions, no record players, just "When can you start?" And this lab had several veterinarians working in it. Veterinarians who decided that rather than going into practice, they were going to research animal diseases. It was a booming field.

Click, clack, click, the puzzle pieces fell into place. I could proceed with my plan and enter the veterinary program, but I would use my degree to pursue research! This seemed like the best of both worlds.

But, as you know, that's not what happened. "The best laid plans of mice and men" and all that. Another accident happened — I fell in love, and that love took me to Winnipeg, where the only realistic option was general practice. There I interviewed for one job where I was told that I would often be left alone, and if I encountered a case that required me to perform an unfamiliar surgery, I was to use the textbooks rather than refer the case elsewhere. Um. No. Yet another interview that did not result in a job.

Ultimately, I ended up at Birchwood as a result of just showing up one day, having decided to hit all the clinics one by one. It was lucky timing as a part-time job had just come open, and the owner apparently took a liking to me. There was no interview, only a perfunctory glance at my resumé and a quick tour of the clinic, followed by a handshake. "Three-month trial basis, two days a week," he said.

Now it's 31 years later. And that was the last time I ever had to look for work. Yes, I'm well aware of how lucky I am.

JAMES AND I

He's back. James Herriot is back. This is a good thing for two reasons. First, the newly rebooted television series, *All Creatures Great and Small*, is delightful. In fact — and I know this will prompt a few indignant letters — it holds its own very well against the beloved original 1978–90 series (both of which are based on his equally beloved books). Second, I will hopefully have to explain myself less frequently now. For someone like me, who grew up in the 1970 and '80s, Herriot was unavoidable. His books had sold 60 million copies worldwide by the time of his death in 1995, and the show developed a cult following. I hadn't read the books — more on this in a bit — or seen the television show, but still I knew who he was, even well before I became interested in veterinary medicine. Everyone in the late 20th century knew who he was. This century? Not so much. I mentioned Herriot in *The Accidental Veterinarian* and one of the young editors told me that she had to look him up, so I should explain to the readers who he was. Hopefully, the new series becomes popular enough that James Herriot is once again a household name, and this story will consequently make more sense to more people.

And what is this story, "James and I"? It's a story of how our lives are oddly dovetailed as well as parallel.

Dovetailed because I entered practice in 1990 just months after he retired. Parallel because we both arrived from elsewhere — James from Scotland, me from Saskatchewan — to start in practice where we didn't know anybody (well, I knew one person — my wife), and we both felt like fish out of water at first. Both of us were at first often viewed with skepticism as too young and too inexperienced. We were both the palest reflections of our legendary, larger-than-life bosses. And speaking of those bosses, both of ours had incendiary tempers that obscured their soft hearts. And then at the other end of our careers, both of us began seriously writing at the age of 50, both having dabbled before.

There things diverge, however. James made a much more serious study of writing than I have, and it shows. It is not false modesty on my part to state that he is the better writer. Some reviews of *The Accidental Veterinarian* helpfully pointed this out — "Schott is a fine writer, but he's no James Herriot." I concur. He casts a long shadow, but it's a cozy place to be, with room for plenty of us. Moreover, his approach to storytelling was different. He wrote *All Creatures Great and Small* like a chronological autobiography, albeit happily admitting that most of the stories were only loosely based on his real experiences and occurred at entirely different times than depicted. The line between fiction and non-fiction is never a sharp one, and there is a lovely art to the blurring. As you well know, I decided on a series of snapshots or vignettes instead, mixed up with respect to the timeline, and varying in style and content, veering erratically from advice, to trivia, to stabs at humour, to shameless tear-jerking. I considered the straight-ahead autobiographical approach, but this would have required more creative "filling in" on my part, and, honestly, I feared even more direct comparisons to *All Creatures Great and Small*. James's books beg to be read by the fireside over a long evening with a mug of tea, or a glass of whisky, or both. I suspect mine are more likely to be picked up, dipped into, and set down again, any time of day, with any beverage. "Apples and oranges," as the saying goes. Or should a veterinarian say, "dogs and cats"? No, that doesn't really work, does it? James wouldn't have tried that.

Where we overlap again is that both of us changed most of the names. In fact, James even changed his own name. His real name was Alf White. My real name is Philipp Schott. I don't expect to become famous enough that this will be a problem.

But James Herriot plays another part in my life. He almost frightened me out of becoming a practising veterinarian. Recall how I wrote that I hadn't read the books or seen the show until much later? This was very unusual for an aspiring vet. As soon I began stumbling down that path, people started asking me, "Have you read James Herriot?" No, that's wrong — they didn't ask, they declared, "You must have read James Herriot!" I hadn't. I hadn't seen the show either because we didn't have cable television, but my excuse for not having read the books was . . . well, I didn't have an excuse. I suppose it never occurred to me. I read a lot, but at that age I mostly read more hardcore non-fiction like histories of medieval Europe, or accounts of mountaineering expeditions to Nepal. As *All Creatures* was starting to feel like an obligation, I got a copy of the omnibus collection of his books from the library and set aside an evening to begin (yes, with tea, but not with whisky, not yet).

I was immediately entranced by the descriptions of the Yorkshire landscape, which may have played a role in the abiding fondness I eventually developed for rural Britain. But I was simultaneously horrified by the descriptions of the job itself. I understood that comparisons to what I was embarking on were ridiculous given that the life of a country vet in the 1930s was as different from the life of a city vet in the 1990s as, well, apples are from oranges, but I was still appalled. Other than a very brief volunteer stint, I had spent no time in a practice, so my mental images of it were gauzy and vague. What James described was dirty, and it was physically hard, and emotionally hard, and populated by all manner of dotty people. Were things really that different now? Fortunately, veterinarians were needed in university research too, and that had been the original plan anyway. Maybe that was the best plan.

But that's not what happened, and I ended up in private practice where I was pleased to learn that the main differences are between country and city practice. Even today, most of what James described applies to the life of a country vet, so hats off to them. In the city, practice is not nearly as dirty or physically hard. It is, however, still emotionally hard, but I've made my peace with that. And the dotty people? That's become one of the best parts of the job. I'm sure that's what James figured out too when he began writing.

KERMIT & FRIENDS

My barber keeps tree frogs as pets. Thus far they have been healthy, but I am girding myself for the day when he asks my advice. I don't know one single thing about tree frog medicine specifically, or even amphibian medicine generally. Within a class of animals one can reasonably extrapolate. From dogs and cats, I can extrapolate to other mammals; from snakes and turtles, I can extrapolate to other reptiles; from budgies and finches, I can extrapolate to other birds, and so on. But I've never had an amphibian as a patient and not one word was expended on them in veterinary school.

So, in preparation for potential forthcoming questions from my barber, I turned to the internet, specifically that subscription database for veterinarians. I set aside an hour to read about tree frogs. The case report headings were intimidating, to say the least:

"Tree Frog with Spindly Leg Syndrome"
"Barking Tree Frog with Corneal Clouding" *(Barking?)*
"Cloacal Prolapse in Alpine Tree Frog"
"Facial Mass in Magnificent Tree Frog"

And, more prosaically:

"Red Leg Syndrome"

I started scanning these articles but soon gave up. At least I now knew the names of a few diseases, but if my barber's frogs ever run into problems, I'll clearly have to do a whole lot more reading. There was no way to reasonably cram enough frog medicine in advance.

I shouldn't have been surprised. This illustrated yet again a basic principle of veterinary medicine: the size of the patient does not correlate to its medical complexity.

This episode reminded me of our one and only amphibian pet, a newt. Before we had cats, or the dog, or children, Lorraine and I had a couple of small freshwater aquariums. One day, browsing in the fish store, we came across a tank of eastern newts. If you don't know what an eastern newt is, picture a greenish-brown salamander the size of your index finger, fetchingly ornamented with rusty red spots.

We were captivated. Fish were all right, but we were eager for a pet who was a little more relatable. Newts have four legs and are one branch closer to us on the tree of life. They also have some kind of weird panache. Some might say personality even. But then some say that about fish too. At the very least, they are easier to project onto than fish.

We called him Mr. Newt, fully aware that he could be a Ms. Newt. We loved having the little guy, and we like to think that he loved living with us. He certainly had more space and less stress than at the pet shop, although this was presumably still a significant downgrade from the wild. But within our capacity to look after him, nothing was too good for our Mr. Newt.

Then one day he vanished.

We lived in a one-bedroom apartment at the time, so we didn't think there were very many places a newt could disappear to. Consequently, we searched with confidence, expecting at any moment to cry out, "There you are Mr. Newt, you little devil you!" as we shook out a shoe or lifted a couch cushion.

But no Mr. Newt. Not anywhere — and we searched everywhere. Twice.

It was as if he had disapparated or beamed himself off the planet. Some people believe that newts possess magical powers. We did not, but we had to wonder where he could possibly be. Had he waited by the door for an opportunity to sneak out when we opened it? But newts move very slowly on land, and then there was the complicating factor of the elevators. We did look up and down the hall, though.

Eventually we stopped looking for and, I must confess, even stopped thinking about Mr. Newt. Life goes on, does it not? The tank was going to be repurposed for more fish and it needed a thorough cleaning. I disassembled the lid, which contained a recessed housing for the light bulbs. The bulbs were crusted with hard water scale, so I unscrewed them to clean them.

There was Mr. Newt.

He was above one of the light bulbs, desiccated like a taco chip. It was heartbreaking to consider that he had boldly decided to break away from the comfort of his routine to seek the light, only to die because of it. There may be a lesson in that. Or not.

I have an appointment with my barber coming up. I plan to avoid the subject of frogs. Fortunately, unlike my last barber who kept futilely trying to draw me into conversation about golf or hockey, this one has broad interests, and we'll manage to fill the half-hour easily without resorting to awkward chat about spindly legs or prolapsed cloacae. However, I might just have to give him the pro tip to check the lights if one of his little guys ever disappears.

THE LAPSE

False modesty is annoying, so I'll spare you that. I'm not going to claim to be stupid; there are many tricks my brain can perform that I'm proud of, but there are also tricks that I wish it would not perform. Like forgetting the simplest things, for example. I am 55 years old as I write this and some younger readers may be smiling and nodding, assuming that forgetfulness is part the natural decline that sets in after, say, 30. Perhaps for some, but I have been absent-minded since I was in kindergarten.

In the early spring of 1970, I was five years old. My kindergarten was in the basement of a church at the corner of Preston and Arlington in Saskatoon. This was only about a kilometre from home, or about a 12-minute walk for a focused adult. In the manner of the time, my mother walked with me once to make sure I knew the way and then after that I was on my own. Happily on my own, it must be said. My five-year-old self had no particular fears or anxieties. That one kilometre along Arlington was an imaginarium of dinosaurs, and knights, and the Arctic, and the high seas, and whatever cartoon I had most recently watched. As is often the case on the Canadian Prairies, we had a false start to spring in early March followed by a blizzard. Kindergarten was closed for a day and when it reopened the parking lot sported a small Mount Everest where the snow had been piled up in a corner. Again, in the manner of the times, after class was dismissed, we were left on our own out there to climb and tumble and throw snowballs. Those who are thinking to themselves "Ah, but it was safer back then" don't know what they're talking about. The murder rate has never been higher than in the early 1970s, pedophiles roamed the land undetected, and massive cars careened about with drunks behind the wheel. *Mad Men* was more documentary than drama. And at a less dramatic level, breaking a bone was a routine rite of passage for a child. But nobody broke anything on our Everest. What happened instead was that I forgot something fundamental. I forgot that cold can really hurt.

Sliding down the snow was fun in our snowsuits, but I thought of a way it could be even more fun (or funner, as I said then). I would take my mittens off and put my indoor running shoes on my hands and then slide down on all fours. It was funner! So much funner that I didn't pay attention to the snow packing into the shoes around my hands. The fun went on and on until most of the kids drifted away. Then I remembered. Snow was cold, and cold can really hurt. I wailed all the way home. The story grew that the odd-shaped knuckles I have on my right hand, at the ends of three fingers, were because of cold damage to the growth plates from that incident. I wonder if that's even possible, but regardless, it was the most pain I had ever experienced to that point. And it was because I was absent-minded.

Thank you for your patience. Here, finally, is the veterinary angle to this story.

Fast-forward 50 years. I'm about to see a new client, Ms. Klassen, and her tiny Yorkshire terrier, Tiana, and I'm about to be absent-minded again. To be sure, I was absent-minded many thousands of times before, but these two episodes are the bookends on an awfully long shelf of such stories.

It was immediately clear that Ms. Klassen was not a person to be trifled with. She was at some indefinite point in middle age, dressed in sharp business attire, and had the look of someone used to judging other people. After 30 years in practice, I'm rarely intimidated anymore, but something about her unblinking stare and coldly polished manner put me on notice. Tiana was similar. She looked freshly groomed, with a red velvet ribbon placed just so on her head, and she refused to take a liver treat. She also stared at me, and I don't think she blinked either.

I busied myself with the examination and perky chit-chat, but both of them continued to pulsate skepticism at my efforts. It probably didn't help matters that I had to step out to find a stethoscope. Most of our exam rooms have one, but I knew this one didn't on that day, and I had forgotten that. But this wasn't the absent-minded lapse yet. And it certainly didn't help when I called her Tatiana rather than Tiana. I was nervous by that point.

That wasn't the lapse either.

"Are you going to examine her eyes?" Ms. Klassen asked, with the faintest whiff of irritation edging her voice.

I had examined them. Or I thought I had. When I don't notice anything unusual the memory doesn't always fully encode.

"Yes, absolutely." I usually go nose to tail and I was checking her hind legs when she asked. I swung back to the front, flicked on the light, and had a(nother?) look.

"They're perfect," I beamed.

"Are you sure? The last doctor said she was prone to glaucoma."

"Oh really? Well, I can measure her eye pressure if you'd like." The appointment had been listed as a routine annual physical, so this would put me behind, but fine, I could do it quickly and get this painful appointment over with.

"Yes, please do." Ice.

"I'll just put a couple anaesthetic drops in first. They'll take ten minutes to work and then I'll come back in and take the pressures."

Ten minutes is an exceedingly long time in a busy veterinary practice. A lot can happen in ten minutes. There's rarely any idle time. There's rarely any standing around, shooting the breeze, waiting for the freezing to kick in time. Ten minutes during an appointment is a gift to get other things done. During that time, I dealt with a phone call, addressed an issue with a hospitalized patient, and checked the testing protocol for something that was coming in later. Then I went into my next appointment.

That was the absent-minded lapse.

That next appointment was long, but routine, and I was on to the following one, a delightful black kitten in for his first shots, when there was a knock on the door. It was a receptionist.

"Ms. Klassen is wondering how long the freezing lasts."

Uh-oh.

It had been 40, possibly 45 minutes. Several thoughts flashed through my head before I replied. The first was that Ms. Klassen was far more patient than I would have given her credit for. The second was that I was an idiot. The third was whether I could slip out the back door, race home, and go into instant early retirement.

I apologized to the kitten's owner, stepped out, and looked at the closed exam room door across the hall, picturing Ms. Klassen on the other side of it. Cold fury incarnate is what I pictured, like one of those Disney villains the moment before they reveal themselves to have supernatural powers of destruction. My hand must have been on the doorknob for a solid four or five seconds while I rehearsed excuses until I came around to what I knew in my heart in the first place: there was no excuse.

Ms. Klassen was still sitting exactly the way she was when I left her, hands folded primly in her lap, ankles crossed, staring straight ahead. Most people would divert themselves with their phones, but if she had, it was put away now. Of the 43 muscles needed to smile, she only used the ones that pulled up the corners of her mouth. The rest of her face was not smiling. Tiana was not smiling either. If anything, she was staring even harder. I have never felt so judged by a dog before.

The freezing had likely begun to wear off, so I reapplied it and stayed in the room, first apologizing a half-dozen different ways, and then becoming manically jolly as I tried to lighten the mood. It was like flicking a Bic at the Ross Ice Shelf in Antarctica. These were the most painful ten minutes I had spent in a long time.

Tiana's eye pressures were normal. I could have cried with relief. Any more time in that room would have killed me.

I don't know whether you believe in karma. I don't really, but sometimes I wonder. My karmic punishment for forgetting to worry about snow packed around my fingers was weird knuckles, and my karmic punishment for forgetting a client in a room was that she inexplicably booked another appointment with me.

THE LAST PET

When I got to work yesterday, there was note asking whether I wanted to write a condolence card for the Miltons. Rosebud had been put to sleep. I closed my eyes and drew in a long breath. I was relieved that one of my colleagues had to perform that euthanasia rather than me — it would have torn my heart out — but I was sad that I would not get a chance to say goodbye to Mrs. Milton. I was quite sure I wouldn't be seeing her again.

I remember the day they brought Rosebud in with a clarity that evades me for many other memories. The Miltons were an elegant elderly couple. They were pleasant, intelligent, well spoken, and both had a great sense of humour. I admired how they looked after their pets, and I admired their relationship as little good-natured barbs and jokes flew back and forth between them. They had series of dogs before Rosebud, but I don't remember anything about them. There might have been a beagle? I don't know. As I said, some memories are clear, and some are just not there. When I put their last dog to sleep, they said, "No more pets. We're too old!" I smiled and replied that I

had often heard that before and gave them 50:50 odds of holding to that vow.

It was only a couple of months later when they reappeared at the clinic with a small pet carrier.

"See, you got a puppy!" I said, beaming.

"No, it's a kitten! We found her in our garden. We watched her for a couple days, putting food out for her, but no mother cat came by. She's so thin!" Mrs. Milton said.

"Oh dear. Well, let's have a look at her then. Are you keeping her?"

"Yes, I think so. We're going to call her Rosebud."

"And we only said we weren't getting another dog! No mention of cats!" Mr. Milton added, laughing.

"No, honey, we said 'no more pets,' not 'no more dogs,' but we're allowed to change our minds for this little sweetheart."

"Ah, but we meant no more dogs!"

"Of course we did, dear. Of course."

They smiled at each other.

I heard a faint meow from inside the carrier. I bent down and saw two green eyes looking back at me. She was a brown tabby, and she had the longest whiskers I think I had ever seen on a kitten.

"I hope you know you've won the lottery, kitty," I thought to myself.

That was 15 years ago. If they were elderly then, they would be very elderly now. Mind you, I was 15 years younger then too, and what I think of as "elderly" has curiously evolved. Regardless, Mrs. Milton had become notably frailer, and Mr. Milton was developing dementia. He hadn't been along for the last few visits, and for the ones prior he had become quieter and quieter, benignly smiling from a chair in the corner of the exam room while his wife did all the talking.

Rosebud really was going to be their last pet. This had been an exceptionally sad euthanasia.

Don't get me wrong, all euthanasias are sad, but some are sadder than others. They are especially sad when the pet is too young, or it's a child's special companion, but among the worst for me are old people's last pets.

Some people just don't want pets anymore because they were originally saddled with them by their kids, or they want to travel now, or are just ready for a different lifestyle, but for many it's the unwelcome end of a wonderful and cherished aspect of their lives. They don't get another pet because they are fearful of what might happen to the animal if they are forced to downsize and cannot find a pet-friendly location. Some also fear they will become unable to properly care for an animal at some point. And many worry about who will look after the pet when they die or need to move into a care home.

That's the part that bothers me. In our society, the last years of our lives are tragically often also the loneliest years. Access to the companionship of an animal should be made easier then, not more difficult. Surely in such a wealthy and sophisticated society we can think of creative solutions to make this possible.

A good start would be to increase the number of pet-friendly apartments and assisted-living accommodations. The trend has unfortunately been going the other way, with more units becoming more restrictive. I'd like someone to show me the data behind these policies. I suspect there is no data. I suspect it's just a "feeling" that pets are somehow too dirty or destructive.

Home care workers often refuse to have anything to do with their patients' pets. This is understandable because they are already overworked and they are not trained in pet care, but in my fantasy world the resources would be there to give the workers time and to train them properly.

A pet can be essential to the well-being of a lonely senior, so it doesn't make sense to ignore that part of their care.

And finally, I don't think it would be difficult to establish networks of volunteers willing to take in pets when the owner has died and no family is available to adopt the animal. These cases touch people's heartstrings. We often have people asking at the clinic if we know of any older pets looking for homes. Having such a network in place would give the elderly some confidence that their pet will be well looked after if something suddenly happens to them.

I don't know whether Mrs. Milton would consider getting another cat if such fears could be addressed. Maybe she was okay with closing that chapter in her life. But maybe I'm wrong in assuming that Rosebud was her last pet. Maybe she will be back with another kitten regardless of all the barriers and worries. I hope so.

LICKY

The other day the kids and I decided that our pets needed superhero names. Unfortunately, however, they don't have any superpowers to base those names on. After some thought we decided to name them after their most impressive vices instead. Superheroes of woe, I suppose. So, Lucy, Gabi, Lillie, and Orbit respectively became Barfo, Licky, Destructo, and Barky. If you have read *How to Examine a Wolverine*, you will have already been treated to the basis of Barfo, Destructo, and Barky's superhero names, but Licky's special super-vice hasn't gotten any attention yet. Now it's her time to shine.

Licky licks her belly bald. It's been going on for years. I would be guessing if I tried to pin down how many, but let's just say "at least five." Licky is 14 years old, so that's a big chunk of her life. She licks it down to a silky pink surface. Sometimes a light fuzz is permitted to grow, but she soon deals with that and it's back to bare skin again. She never licks to the point of irritating the skin, nor does she lick past the customary bounds. It's always the same symmetrical rectangle with rounded corners in her lower abdomen. There's a touching neatness to it. Some animals have skin conditions where they lick and scratch themselves in a chaotic frenzy, pockmarking their coat with random bald patches. This looks terrible and must feel terrible. Only a negligent owner would leave their pet to suffer like that without seeking medical help. Licky's licking, on the other hand, was subdued, slow, and only occasional — just enough to keep that specific patch bare. No more, no less. She never seems distressed, only intent and highly focused, like a person absorbed in a favourite hobby requiring finesse, like, say, putting ships in bottles.

This odd behaviour is relatively common and goes by several names. Usually, we call it overgrooming or self-barbering, but there are more scientific names too and these depend on what we think the cause is. This is where things get tricky, because the exact same mild chronic belly licking can have three very different causes.

According to the literature, a large majority of cats like Licky have allergies and are itchy as a result. Usually, the allergy is to something in the environment, such as house dust (plenty enough of that around here . . .), in which case we would call it atopic dermatitis. I specified "according to the literature" because my own experience has been different. We have access to excellent allergy medications, and I find that in at least half of overgrooming cases these make no difference. So it was with Licky. She kept right on licking, even though the drugs should have gotten rid of the itch. I wonder whether in some of these cases it starts as an allergy, then the allergy goes away, but the behaviour persists out of habit. Regardless, at this point we now have a behavioural issue, and would therefore call it psychogenic alopecia. Those neat rectangles are a clue that this is a type of obsessive-compulsive disorder. It appears to be caused by stress and is most common in the more anxious cats. It reminds me of people chewing their fingernails or twiddling neurotically with their hair. The laid-back, sociable, super-chill Garfield variety of cat rarely overgrooms. It's almost always the jumpy, flighty ones who disappear the second a strange person enters the house. Licky is definitely one of those. When we travel, we have someone come to the house twice a day to look after the cats. She often won't see Licky for the entire time we're away. She's the ghost cat. More legend than reality.

The third cause has only been relatively recently discovered. It seems that some cats with certain bladder or bowel issues will be drawn to lick at the overlying skin as a self-soothing behaviour. That would explain the weirdly specific location of the licking. This can end up being a bit circular, though, as the bladder and bowel issues involved are also often related to stress.

What can be done? Or, better yet, what should be done? If you have addressed any allergies and bladder or bowel issues, or ruled them out, you can try a barrier. By this I mean a lampshade-style "Elizabethan collar," or "e-collar." People try little t-shirts too, but they can usually get around those. An e-collar works. It is something that *can* be done, but *should it*?

I'm going to express an unpopular opinion. Some in my profession believe that no cat should be allowed to overgroom. But we've allowed Licky to keep licking because she has passed the two tests I set for this situation. The first is, is she harming herself? The answer is no. If she were irritating the skin, it would be different, but she isn't. The second is, is it causing her significant distress? The answer to that is also no. If she were constantly licking, or even doing it several times a day for prolonged periods, or if it interfered with her ability to eat, sleep, play, and generally be a normal, happy (if neurotic) cat, then we would do something. But it doesn't. It's a vice. Should people who chew their nails down to the quick wear gloves all day and night to prevent this? Maybe, if it were just for a few days, but you know that won't work. They'd have to wear them for months, and even then the likelihood of relapse would be high. And so it is with e-collars. They are distressing and inconvenient to wear, which is acceptable for the short term and for something serious like preventing stitches from being removed, but is it really on balance the right thing to do for something chronic and mild? It's a classic case of the cure being worse than the disease. So Licky is allowed to lick. One of life's innumerable little compromises.

And the name didn't stick. She quickly reverted to being lovable old Gabi. Who among us wants to be defined by our vices? What would your superhero name be if it were based on your chief vice? I know what mine would be, and I'm not telling you.

LUMPY

It usually goes like this. A client enters the exam room with an elderly Labrador retriever. It doesn't have to be a Lab, but it often is. Both look nervous. The Lab relaxes once you give her a few liver treats. The client does not. The client then explains that they have found a new lump on their dog. He tries to sound casual, but he is tense. A lump means cancer. In his mind, he knows there are probably many kinds of lumps that are not cancerous, but in his heart, he dreads that this one is. The neighbour's dog had a mysterious lump, and then it died. Same with the cat he had growing up — lump found, then dead. Ditto for his aunt. Lumps are no good.

But I smile and my smile is genuine, not just put-on professionally mandated optimism. Far more lumps in dogs are benign than you fear, and far more of them are just fat than you imagine. So, I palpate the lump and, sure enough, it is deep under the skin, smooth, loose, oval, and rubbery. A classic lipoma. I need to rule out a rare mast cell tumour that can pretend to be a lipoma, but otherwise, this is not a worry. The client finally relaxes. The Lab continues to stare at the treat jar.

So, what exactly is a lipoma, you ask? The answer is in the name. The "lip" means fat, as in lipids or liposuction, and the "oma" means tumour, as in sarcoma, carcinoma, lymphoma and, with apologies to my lovely grandmothers, all the other lumpy omas. But "tumour" does not imply death-dealing malignancy. It just means that cells have divided more than they should have and have formed a lump. So long as the lump plays nice and doesn't send colonists into vital organs, we call it benign. And lipomas always play nice.

Some lipomas, however, don't know when to stop growing. It's still playing nice and not threatening the health or life of the patient, but it's making the patient look funny or, depending on where it is, walk funny. The great majority don't get much bigger than a walnut, but a small number will keep growing, to lemon, orange, and even grapefruit sizes. And a very small number make the leap from citrus to sports and keep growing to volleyball, soccer ball, or basketball sizes. They're still not painful or deadly at this size, but they are certainly awkward, and possibly even embarrassing. "He's growing another dog!" is a common joke. No dog ever laughed at that.

Fortunately, lipomas are usually easy to remove. I don't recommend an operation for the nut- or smaller citrus-sized ones since it isn't worth the stress of surgery for the patient, and it can be like a game of whack-a-mole where you take one off only to see another sprout somewhere else in a couple months. The awkward ones, however, should be operated on.

Here's a gross fact. (Feel free to skip to the next paragraph.) Most lipomas are easy to remove, even when large, because they "shell out." This means that they have minimal attachment to the rest of the body and can essentially be scooped out by the surgeon's fingers once the skin incision is made. They scoop out in a single jiggly blob and are often compared to breast implants. I suppose that's actually two gross facts; sorry. A few do not shell out nicely because they arise from the fat within a muscle and are thus intertwined with it. Those are just "debulked" and will eventually grow back to their previous size. Incidentally, to clear up one common misconception, lipomas are not caused by being overweight, and are no more likely in obese dogs than thin dogs. They are just caused by age.

Most clients make their peace with the growing lumpiness of their aging dogs, but a few are still bothered by it. Even once they are assured that there is no malignancy, the lumps continue to trouble them. I used to secretly think that was silly, but I get it now. Orbit, our nine-year-old Sheltie, has begun to sprout lipomas. First one, then two. Initially peanut-sized, then almond, and now walnut. Actually, I think I'm fooling myself. The transition from nuts to citrus has probably already occurred. However, this has allowed me to understand how it feels vaguely disturbing when you stroke your lumpy dog. This is partly aesthetic — ooh, he used to be so smooth and sleek — but it's also partly emotional. It's a sign of aging, a sign of deterioration. It's like the first time you really clue in to the fact that your parents have become old. Knowing that it is inevitable and natural doesn't make it any easier to accept. But we accept it anyway, as hard as it is. My lumpy old boy, your lumpy old girl — they may be lumpy on the outside, but they're still the same smooth and sleek loves of our lives on the inside.

MAKING THE DUCK SOUND

What does a duck say? Go ahead, say it. Out loud, if you dare. "Quack, quack," right?

I wish, oh how I wish, that I had another duck tale for you, but the only two ducks I have had the good fortune to treat have already made their way into my first and second books. Alas, there is no third duck to grace this third book. No, instead I'm referring to the duck's quack's homonym, the medical quack. Incidentally, in case you're curious, the two uses for "quack" are a linguistic coincidence. In the Netherlands in the 17th century, a "kwakzalver" was a peddler of home remedies. It lost the "zalver" in its transit over the English Channel and the spelling was anglicized — i.e., made more irrational — hence quack. Technically, quackery is fraudulent and consciously dishonest. For the purposes of this story, I am using a gentler definition wherein the quack is simply ignorant of the obsolescence of his treatments. He is not trying to hoodwink his clients; he just doesn't know any better.

In my first few years in practice, I encountered a few veterinarians who made the duck sound and I vowed as fervently as I could that I would never allow myself to become that way. But as time has gone on, I have become a little more empathetic to those old guys. I certainly hope that I am not making duck sounds myself, but it's easy to see how it can happen.

Imagine, if you will, spending years at university learning your profession's state-of-the-art practices. You do this day in, day out, day after day, month after month, year after year. Your brain is full. It is so up to date, it gleams. It might even have that new-car smell (new-brain smell?). Then you graduate. And as soon as that happens, the gas pedal hits the floor without you even touching it, and you and your brain accelerate into the future. School quickly recedes in the rear-view mirror until it disappears entirely behind the horizon. Your knowledge, once so shiny, once so new, begins to accumulate grime. The road is bumpy and you're moving fast, so some parts even fall off.

We try our best to service our brains, but you know how it is. You can change the oil religiously, you repair every problem the moment you notice it, you treat it as gently as you can, but it's never the same as new.

I apologize. I'm mixing my metaphors. Ducks and cars. Is sloppy use of metaphors the writer's version of quackery? Perhaps. Anyway, let me bring this back to the real for a moment. We have journals to read, online databases to check, colleagues to chat with, and conferences to attend, but you would have to do these things full time to be as up to date as you were when you graduated. For the most part, this is more than compensated for by the benefits of experience. If medicine were just the black-and-white application of knowledge — symptom A means disease B resulting in treatment C — then anyone with an internet connection could become a doctor. Often symptom A could be a whole alphabet of diseases, leading to another alphabet of treatment options, none of which work in every patient every time, even if you have the diagnosis right. Experience is what allows us to develop the judgment needed to know what is most likely wrong with this specific patient, and what will most likely benefit them. But you still need to know what diagnoses and what treatments are available. New diseases are described regularly, and new treatments seem to appear almost daily. If by chance you didn't attend the right conference or have time to read the right journal at the right moment, then you could miss these. Over time you can miss more and more of these and, sadly, begin to make the duck sound without even knowing you're doing it.

This is where colleagues are helpful. The other day I performed a cardiac ultrasound on an old cocker spaniel for a veterinarian across town. After he received the report, he called me to get my opinion on treatment options. I described what I would do if Benny were my patient. My colleague paused for a moment and then asked whether I had read the updated American College of Veterinary Internal Medicine consensus guidelines regarding mitral valve disease. I confessed that I had not. I was unaware that a new version had come out. *(Insert the duck sound.)* He was kind about it and we both laughed, but I felt foolish and abashed.

That's how easily it can happen. For something as important as heart disease I would have found out one way or another fairly quickly, but how many patients would miss the optimal treatment in the meantime? To be fair, not all new treatment approaches are true improvements, and over the years I have seen more than one come full circle back around to the previous way of doing things, but for those single steps backwards there are always at least four going forwards. If you rest on your laurels (gadzooks, a third metaphor!), satisfied that what you've always done works pretty well, then you have in fact let the transmission slip into reverse. You're looking in that rear-view mirror towards old knowledge. While quacking. And while wearing a wreath of laurel leaves askew on your head, like some sort of frazzled ancient Greek athlete. Picture that. Not a pretty sight, is it?

It's fun to say "quack," but it's not fun to be one.

MARIGOLD

I can be shallow. Take for example the fact that while I do love all my patients (yes, even the snarly ones — it's rarely, if ever, their fault), I love some more than others, and sometimes this is for shallow, self-centred reasons. Marigold was one of these. I especially loved her not only because she was objectively a good dog, and because all dogs are worthy of love anyway, but because she was a miniature version of my dog, Orbit. In fact, the staff called her "Mini-Orbit." Marigold was a Shetland sheepdog, like Orbit, with the exact same beautiful sable markings, but she was half his size. She also had his sweet and stoic disposition, although that sweetness and stoicism clearly hid a mischievous streak.

Marigold presented to me because she had become weak and lethargic, and she was having some difficulty urinating. On examination she had arthritis in her elbows, but this didn't explain the symptoms. Arthritic dogs are stiff or lame, not weak and lethargic. So, we ran the usual battery of basic tests. Everything was normal, other than some red blood cells in the urine. A bladder infection was presumed. Usually these also show white blood cells on a urine test, but not always. The weakness and lethargy didn't fit with a bladder infection either, but it was all we had to go on then, so it seemed reasonable to try antibiotics and see what would happen.

She didn't improve. She didn't really get worse, but she didn't improve either. I asked her family to bring her back in for an ultrasound, fearing that perhaps there was a cancer producing the red blood cells. That would explain the other symptoms as well.

Marigold lay there for her ultrasound, staring straight ahead, not tense, but not relaxed either. It was like she had focused all her attention on an imaginary distant flock of sheep. The ultrasound was clean — no tumours or any other visible pathology. This was a relief, but it begged the question, what was going on here?

Then I had an idea. I put my ultrasound probe away and got out an exam glove and lubricant — I was going to perform a rectal examination. Two-thirds of the urethra (the tube leading from the bladder to the vagina) is not visible on ultrasound because the pelvic bones get in the way. However, on rectal examination you can feel that part of the urethra like a fat thread under your finger, between the rectum and the floor of the pelvis.

Marigold continued to stare at her imaginary sheep as I did this, only raising her eyebrows ever so slightly.

My fears were confirmed — she had a urethral tumour the size of a shelled peanut. At least urethral tumours were usually not that aggressive and could sometimes be made to shrink with simple anti-inflammatory medications. The tumour explained the continued presence of blood in the urine despite antibiotics, but it did not explain the lethargy.

Then I had another idea. Shelties are prone to poor thyroid function, which can make them weak and lethargic. Many will also gain weight and have skin problems, neither of which applied to Marigold, but, as we like to say, "the dogs don't read the textbooks." There are exceptions to almost any medical norm. And sure enough, Marigold was hypothyroid. Hurray! Of course, I never wish a disease on a patient, but this was one that was easy to treat and would make a big difference to how she felt.

But it didn't. Marigold's urination improved a little on the anti-inflammatory, but she was steadily becoming even weaker, despite being on thyroid medication. This always worked, so I had been excited to make the follow-up call. For every other hypothyroid patient, the owners used words like "miracle" and "amazing." But not for Marigold. The owners, a lovely middle-aged couple, were very patient and understanding. You could hear the quaver of emotion in their voices when we discussed possible bad scenarios, but they were dedicated to doing whatever they could for their sweet Marigold. Struggling to think of reasonable options, I increased the dose of thyroid medication.

Still nothing.

Marigold came back for yet another recheck. Now she was barely walking. The one thing we hadn't done yet was to x-ray her. Ultrasound provides a far more detailed view of all the abdominal structures, but it is blind to bone. In particular, in a patient losing the ability to walk, the spine becomes a focus. To my horror, there it was — a tumour in her lower spine. Her urethral tumour was probably one of the rare ones that had spread metastatically. The hypothyroidism, although real, was a coincidence, a red herring.

There was no hope for Marigold. We could control any pain she felt, but we couldn't help her walk. Surgery wasn't an option. Although it broke their hearts, Marigold's people knew they didn't have a choice. One snowy winter morning they met me in the parking lot and, sobbing, handed her to me, bundled in a blanket with her favourite plush toy. They couldn't face coming in to watch her be put to sleep. I carried her in, my eyes blurring with tears. Marigold ignored me, and looked straight ahead, hopefully seeing her sheep.

Forgive me, but I love some of my patients more than others.

OLD DOG LESSONS

The title is misleading. The dog giving the lessons, Orbit, is not "old." Naturally, he is showing some signs of aging,

but that is of course a constant process, right from birth. We all only stop aging when we die. As I write this, he is eight and a half years old — "middle-aged," let's say. I won't think of him as old until he's in the double digits, which is only a year and a half away. But let's not dwell on that. For now, he's still middle-aged, but "Middle-Aged Dog Lessons" doesn't have the same ring.

As an aside, this is a good time to address a top ten question asked of vets: "How old is my dog in people years?" There used to be an easy way to answer this, but unfortunately it was wrong. We used to simply multiply by seven, and presto, there was your answer. A ten-year-old dog was 70, which sort of almost maybe made sense back when most dogs were lucky to see their teens. But that rare 20-year-old Chihuahua was 140! Amazing. Even more amazing was the routine fact of puppies going into the equivalent of puberty at six months of age, or three and a half human years! Imagine your toddler's voice cracking and a wispy moustache appearing on his upper lip. Or needing a training bra and feminine hygiene products. But we cheerfully ignored these quirks of the "seven times" math for decades. Now we know better. Now we do something much more complicated. Are you ready? Here's the formula:

At 1 a dog is 15 in human years.

At 2 a dog is 24 in human years.

After that, add 5 human years for every dog year for most dogs, but add 4 for very small dogs, and 6 for giant breeds.

Got it?

(Incidentally, if you're doing the cat age math, the formula is the same, with cats equating to small dogs.)

So, by this formula, eight-and-a-half-year-old Orbit is $24 + [(8.5 - 2) \times 5] = 56.5$. That 20-year-old Chihuahua is now $24 + [(20 - 2) \times 4] = 96$. And sadly, a 12-year-old Newfoundlander is already $24 + [(12 - 2) \times 6] = 84$. By the way, I hope all those nesting brackets haven't given any of you math anxiety flashbacks. If you prefer, the charts are easy to find on the internet.

But Orbit is, like I said, middle-aged. In fact, at 56.5, he's only a year older than I am right now. He passed me late last fall sometime.

Consider the foregoing a bonus story. It was not what I intended to write about. I intended to write about what Orbit is teaching me as he ages.

I'm not a nickname kind of guy. A small number of people — none of them family or close friends — call me "Phil," but that's a contraction, not a nickname. One classmate back in veterinary school tried "Flip" on for size, but that didn't stick. However, when I worked for Dr. Bruce Murphy over several summers while in university, he started calling me "Flying Phil" and that became widespread among the graduate students in his endocrinology lab.

Bruce had noticed a fundamental truth about me. I am quick. I walk quickly, I talk quickly, and I eat quickly. I consciously try to slow down the latter two because I know that they are not good things. The walking quickly is mostly positive, unless I'm walking with my family and annoying them by constantly surging ahead, but the talking and eating are problems. Yet, despite knowing this, and despite decades now of trying to slow down, my default is still to be quick. I've made my peace with who I am, but that doesn't mean I don't want to keep trying.

Orbit is helping now. He's still an energetic dog and can easily keep pace with me, when he wants to, but since becoming middle-aged, increasingly he doesn't want to. When I say, "Do you want to go for a walk, Orbit?" he hears, "Do you want to go for a sniff, Orbit?" Like most dogs, he's always been an enthusiastic sniffer, but in the last couple years this has apparently turned into his life's primary mission. Whereas a simple tug on the leash used to be enough to stop him from sniffing and get him walking again, now I have to yank hard, and drag him. Literally. He puts on the brakes by bracing his legs and leaning away from me, and he adopts what I can only describe as a stubborn facial expression. As I haul, the collar rides up against the back of his head, pushing the fur forward, and he locks his legs in position. I'm bigger and stronger, so I win, but at a cost. Orbit is disgruntled. People stare. I feel judged. I want Orbit to enjoy his sniffing, but, damn it, even more so, I just want to go!

Then slowly I started giving in more frequently. Orbit took full advantage of this, creating a feedback loop wherein he tried stopping even more, and I gave in even more, to the point that some of our walks now consist mostly of meandering and sniffing. None of this high-velocity arrow-straight ambulation. For a smell connoisseur, that must be like power-walking through the Louvre. Sure, you're getting exercise, but you're missing all the best stuff! When I have a busy day, this is as painful as getting in the slowest checkout line at the grocery store. Mindfulness experts will tell you to actively seek these situations out. It's easy to be mindful at the beach or during a yoga class, but for true practice, pick something that would normally frustrate you and make you impatient. So they say. Orbit, as it turns out, is a mindfulness master. Most animals are. I am trying to learn from him. While he slows down to smell the pee, I'm trying to slow down and smell the roses (mostly metaphorical, especially during the winter). Incidentally, I originally planned to title this story, "Slow Down and Smell the Pee," but I didn't want people to skip it.

Now, when I want to walk quickly with Orbit, because I still prefer that and because he still can keep up, I pick routes that take us across as many open fields as possible. He still finds the occasional apparently well-perfumed blade of grass that requires deep sniffing, but otherwise we're able to go straight and fast and far, neither of us old in any way.

OUT OF THE WILD

It's almost always a shoebox. Even the tiniest pets are brought in cages or special travel carriers, but wildlife always arrives in shoeboxes. It could be a squirrel, or a rabbit, or a wild bird. Usually, the shoebox is held by a child, the child having shamed their parent into picking up the injured animal and taking it to the vet. The shoebox will have holes punched in it for air and will be carefully lined with paper towel. Often there'll be some sort of food placed in it — whatever the child and parent thought the animal might like. This food is never eaten.

I wrote about an orphaned baby bunny in *The Accidental Veterinarian*, and I wrote about rescued squirrels in *How to Examine a Wolverine*. But wild birds deserve a story of their own. I have seen many, oh so many, and I'll tell you right up front that there are not a lot of happy endings. But you didn't pick up this book to get bummed out (I'm sorry about the Marigold story), so I'll dig deep and recount one of the exceptions.

The shoebox was red. I don't recall the brand. And yes, it was brought in by a small child accompanied by her embarrassed father. He exuded a "you and I both know this is a complete waste of time, but let's humour the kid" vibe. But I didn't know that it was a complete waste of time. To be sure, as mentioned above, most of these bird-in-a-box situations do not turn out well, but every now and again one does, and I am fundamentally an optimist; a glass is 5% full kind of guy.

I thanked the child for being so caring and asked her to place the box on the reception counter. I cautiously lifted one corner. More than once I've been told that a bird can't fly, only to find it miraculously healed and in a tremendous hurry to leave. Once we had a sparrow flitting about the wards for the better part of the day before it became exhausted enough to allow itself to be caught.

This bird did not try to fly. In fact, it lay there, motionless on the paper towel, and did not react when I looked in. It was what the birdwatchers call an "LBJ," or "little brown job." In other words, one of dozens of barely distinguishable species of small brown birds. I certainly had no idea.

"Is he going to be okay?" the child asked.

"I hope so, but I don't know yet."

I opened the box a little farther, hoping that (a) the bird wasn't dead already, and (b) that it wasn't faking it and planning to rocket out, flapping hysterically past my face. I leaned in and looked more closely. It was breathing.

"Well, he's breathing, so that's a good sign," I said, lamely.

"Can you help him?"

"Maybe. Sometimes all they need is time to heal. Do you know what happened to him?"

"He flew into our window."

The father shrugged, as if to say, "Yeah, it happens."

It does. One study pegged the number of annual bird window strike deaths at one billion in the USA alone. At flap.org, a charity dedicated to reducing these deaths, a counter in the top corner starts running as soon you arrive at their website. Within seconds the number of birds who died in collisions with buildings during my visit was in the four figures. It made me want to leave the site quickly, which I don't think was their intent. Their logo is a dead bird. Another questionable choice, but they do excellent work and deserve our support.

I looked at the unfortunate bird again. He (or she) still wasn't moving, but the upside was that I could therefore perform a simple examination. I carefully picked him up, cupped in my right hand. It was like picking up something that was weightless, yet somehow also warm and soft. With my left hand I gently extended each wing. Nothing broken. I looked for signs of bleeding. Also nothing. I gingerly touched his skull and neck, not sure what I was expecting to determine, but that felt normal too.

"Well, there's nothing obvious. Hopefully, he's just stunned. We'll put him in a dark and quiet place and see how he does."

"I hope he gets better. Poor bird," the girl said.

"I have a feeling he'll be fine," I said.

I don't know why I said that. I hardly ever talk about feelings or intuition when it comes to medical matters such as prognosis. I will say that the odds are good, or that they're bad, or 50/50, but that's based on a rational analysis of the available information rather than instinct or any other subconscious machinations. Anything that hints at superstition or unscientific thinking makes me squirm. Whenever a staff member claims that it will be a crazy day because it's a full moon, I can be counted on to declare, "Nonsense! We're a science-based profession!"

I put the red shoebox and its stunned occupant in the far corner of an otherwise unused ward, turned off the light, and left him alone.

The day turned into a hectic blur of appointments, procedures, and phone calls. I was exhausted by the end of the day and happy to put my jacket on and head for the back door. I had just placed my hand on the doorknob when one of the technologists ran down the hall to catch up with me.

"Philipp! Before you go, what do you want us to do with that bird?"

Shoot. The bird. I had completely forgotten about him.

"Oh, yeah. Right! Thanks for reminding me. Let's have a look at him."

I didn't need to open the lid. As soon as we turned the light on, there was a scrabbling sound from inside the shoebox. When I picked the box up, I could hear both the scritch-scratch of little bird toenails on the cardboard and the soft rapid thwack-thwack of wings hitting the sides.

"Let's take him outside."

I reasoned that if he were ready to fly, it might as well be directly to freedom, and if he wasn't, it would be easy to catch him and return him to the clinic for more rest.

He was ready to fly. As soon as the lid was half open, he shot out. He was initially uncoordinated and briefly flopped onto the grass but then, with a few strong wing-beats, he was properly airborne. Without a glance back he took off in a straight line down the back lane, rising above the power poles. We soon lost sight of him. I can only imagine the stories he'll tell his friends.

So, my feeling was right, and the little girl was right to bring him in to recover in the clinic, out of reach of prowling cats. It doesn't always work out that way, but when it does, it's wonderful.

PARKING LOT MEDICINE

Let's start with a brief geography lesson. I live in Winnipeg, Canada. Winnipeg is relatively far south by Canadian standards, close to the US border, but Arctic air often makes its most southerly excursion here because of the proximity of Hudson Bay. Consequently, Winnipeg routinely makes its way onto lists of the "coldest cities on Earth." This is also reflected in its gently mocking nickname, "Winterpeg." In recent years Winnipeggers have embraced this identity with more genuine enthusiasm, but the factual reality of the cold remains. In January it is not uncommon to have stretches of weeks where the temperature does not exceed −20 Celsius (−4 Fahrenheit), and once the wind is factored in, it's possible for it to feel like −40 Celsius (also −40 Fahrenheit). In case you've never experienced this, rest assured that it is as cold as it sounds. However, usually when it's that cold it's also sunny and the humidity is low. What can I say? You get used to it. I'm fond of quoting the English explorer Sir Ranulph Fiennes, who said, "There is no such thing as bad weather, only inappropriate clothing." It's true. I happily walk to work in these conditions. But it takes me a solid ten minutes to get all my gear on. Only deep sea and outer space involve more complicated preparation.

Now that you know it is very cold here, you can begin to form a picture of this story based on the title. I just read the other day that Germans have coined 1,200 new words in relation to the COVID-19 pandemic, mostly consisting of bracingly long compound confections. I'm not sure about new words, but veterinarians have coined several new phrases in English as well. "Parking lot medicine" is one of them. Perhaps German vets say "Parkplatzmedicin."

The pandemic has meant locked doors for most clinics. The nature of our work involves close engagement with people as they hold their pets while we examine them. Early studies indicated that veterinarians and their staff were in one of the highest risk categories for COVID-19 infection. In response, most of us put new systems in place on the fly. Clients would remain in the parking lot and phone in on arrival. Concerns and history would be collected over the phone, and then a staff member, or the veterinarian, would go out to the parking lot to collect the pet. The pet would be examined in the clinic, and then the veterinarian would phone the client to discuss treatment options. Treatment would proceed and the pet would be brought back out to the car afterwards.

That was the theory.

The reality was that the phone lines were often busy, or the client didn't answer their cellphone, or on picking up the pet at the car the client had several more questions, or it just seemed easier, more efficient, and frankly friendlier to go out and chat in the parking lot. The pandemic began here in March, as spring was getting underway. All the toing and froing from the parking lot took time, but it worked reasonably well. We admitted to each other that it was kind of nice to get out of the often circus-like atmosphere of the clinic to be outside in the sun and spring breeze for a few minutes, and we quickly settled into this new routine. Summer came and went, and then fall as well. We had a long, dry, and relatively warm fall. But winter comes every year. Sometimes in late October already, sometimes not until mid-December, but most commonly at some point in November, the temperature drops off a cliff and the world turns white overnight. The latter is welcome as November is usually otherwise a dreary brown and grey, but the former creates practical issues. Chief among these, for the purposes of this discussion, is talking to clients in the parking lot.

When it is warm, clients will often get out of their cars and we will then both stand in the warm sun, safely distanced, and talk about their pet. This is pleasant. When it is cold, clients will stay in their cars and we'll talk through the partially opened window. Usually, all the important information has been discussed over the phone in advance, so this is a very brief exchange, but sometimes the client remembers something else they want to talk about before I take their pet into the clinic. This is unpleasant.

Me: "Hi, is that Buffy?"

The air temperature is -25 and the forecast is for increasing wind. My hands are in my pockets and my shoulders are hunched, but I'm only going to be out here a few seconds, so it's fine.

Client: "Yes, it is!"

Me: "I'm Dr. Philipp Schott! We just spoke on the phone. I'll bring Buffy inside for her checkup now. I'll call you if I have any questions."

The client rolls their window down a little farther but doesn't seem to be in a hurry to get Buffy, who is curled up on the passenger seat.

The wind begins to pick up. I hunch my shoulders further.

Client: "Okay, but I'm supposed to ask you one thing first."

Me: "Sure!" I smile broadly. I'm hardy in the cold. One thing. Whatever.

The client digs in a jacket pocket and then rummages in the glove compartment before trying a different jacket pocket. "Sorry, Doctor, my wife gave me a note." More digging and rummaging. "Ah, here it is." He begins to carefully unfold a sheet of yellow note paper with a cartoon bee in the top right corner.

The wind is really sharp now. I'm still smiling, but my lips are freezing, so there is an increasingly unnatural rigidity to my smile. I extend my hand to take the note, but it seems the client wishes to read it out to me. I put my hand back in my pocket and stamp my feet involuntarily. The client does not appear to notice.

Client: "Please ask the vet to check the three lumps on her back, and ask him about the funny smell she has, and make sure to look in her ears, and . . ."

This is not "one thing." The tip of my nose and the tops of my ears are becoming painful. The wind picks up further, whipping little ice pellets off a nearby snowdrift. I tuck my chin into my neck and begin to shiver.

". . . ask him if she really needs all those shots at her age, and . . ."

I'm tuning him out now. The weather office said that exposed flesh will freeze in under a minute. I think I've been out here an hour now. Subjectively, that is. But even objectively, it's been well over a minute and I suspect my extremities will turn bone white and fall off shortly, making a glassy tinkling sound as they hit the ground.

And then, miraculously, he stops talking, opens the door, and starts fussing with his seatbelt so that he can climb out, slowly walk around the car, open the passenger door, and carefully get Buffy out for me.

Client: "Do you want the note?"

Me, through literally chattering teeth: "Yes, please."

And of course, Buffy was very reluctant to walk towards the clinic and had to be coaxed, and of course, the door had been accidentally locked, so I had to wait until a staff member could respond to the frantic knocking (and plaintive cries). But eventually I escaped the parking lot and, as you can see, lived to tell the tale.

Now it is spring again and by next winter, with any luck whatsoever, we'll all be vaccinated, and the parking lot medicine of 2020–21 will be a distant, weird memory.

A closing thought on the parking lot medicine story: too many people drive black SUVs. I cannot count the number of times the staff has told me that a client is in a "black

SUV" only to find that there a half-dozen such vehicles in the parking lot. What's wrong with the other colours? What's wrong with sedans, coupes, hatchbacks, station wagons, minivans, sports cars, convertibles, etc.? Sigh. I apologize — I'm not normally this cranky. COVID is hard in entirely unexpected ways.

PARROTOSAURUS

I'm game to see just about any species. As readers of my previous books will recall, I've examined pythons, wolverines, and poisonous lionfish, among other odd beasts. But I won't see parrots. This is not due to a lack of interest or a strange bias, but rather it is due to a lack of knowledge and a lack of courage.

When it comes to pythons, wolverines, and poisonous lionfish, I am much like the man in the parable where in the land of the blind, the one-eyed man is king. I may not know much, but the little bit I know is still more than most. This is decidedly not the case when it comes to parrots and other fancy birds. If you haven't put hundreds of hours into familiarizing yourself with the medical peculiarities well known to bird specialists, you run the risk of replicating Monty Python's "Dead Parrot" sketch. This would not only be a heartbreaking mistake, but an expensive one. These birds can easily cost \$10,000 or more. Happily, I do not need to try to be a one-eyed king as I have several colleagues in the city who are fully two-eyed when it comes to birds, so there's no reason to bring your parrot to me. Moreover, most parrot owners are extremely knowledgeable themselves. I don't mind looking foolish among friends for entertainment purposes, but when it comes to my professional life, I like to avoid it. Call it pride, or something.

So that's my lack of parrot knowledge. Lack of courage has to do with the beak. Yes, of course, my other patients mostly have teeth and teeth can do bad things to you as well, but I have learned how to tell when something is planning to bite me. Parrots are much more mysterious, and that beak is frankly terrifying. For a spot of grisly fun I suggest you perform an internet search for "can a parrot bite your finger off." A website called Beak Craze states that "Very few birds can bite hard enough to take off fingers in adult humans." Very few? I am not feeling reassured. It then goes on to say, "Generally speaking, a cockatoo can cause a bad crushing injury and nerve damage, but it is unlikely to remove the entire finger." Still not feeling reassured.

Here's the thing about birds — they are dinosaurs. I mean this in the literal biologically correct sense. When I was a child, we believed that modern reptiles like lizards and crocodiles were the direct descendants of dinosaurs. Green and scaly and cold-blooded, how could they not be? However, it turns out that dinosaurs were probably not green and scaly and cold-blooded. Many dinosaurs were colourful, some had primitive feathers for sexual display, and some were likely warm-blooded. Like birds. And then detailed study of the skeletal anatomy sealed the deal. Dinosaurs did not go extinct. The giant ones did. But the small ones continued to evolve and are all around us today. That sweet little sparrow at your bird feeder? Dinosaur. That comical chicken in the barnyard? Dinosaur. And that parrot eyeing me from across the exam table. Definitely dinosaur.

Knowing this becomes a trick of perspective. Watch how any bird moves across the ground with its head bobbing slightly and softly say to yourself, "Dinosaur, dinosaur, dinosaur." It'll be like one of those Magic Eye pictures and suddenly you'll see it. And when you do, you'll say, "Dinosaur, dinosaur . . . holy Toledo!" and take a step backwards. At least that's what I did when it first clicked for me. Not so sweet and innocent-looking anymore, eh? Don't get me wrong, I love birds. In fact, I have a strong suspicion that I'm on the path to becoming a dotty old bird-watcher when I retire. I even have the Tilley hat already. It's that I now have more respect for birds. Appearances are always so deceptive. Beautiful doesn't mean gentle, and cute doesn't mean passive.

Back to that parrot eyeing me from across the exam table. Somehow Sultan had made it through the screening process and been booked with me. I think it might have been a new receptionist who was told that "Dr. Schott sees everything" without the important caveat being explained.

Sultan was a magnificent hyacinth macaw. He was a shade of dazzling blue that made him look freshly painted, or like a cartoon character, with bright yellow highlights around his eyes and edging his beak.

His beak.

For some reason that probably falls somewhere between masochism and paranoia, before going into the exam room to see Sultan I looked up the strength of the average hyacinth macaw's beak. 200 pounds of pressure per square inch (1,378,951 pascals!). Enough to snap a broomstick. Enough to crack a coconut. Enough to . . . well, you get the idea.

Sultan was also enormous. Perched on the owner's shoulder, his head was above hers and his tail feathers extended past her elbow. He regarded me with what I can only describe as a beady eye. Like a dinosaur. His expression was . . . I had no idea what his expression was. Mammals, I can read. Birds and dinosaurs, not so much. Was that his "pleased to meet you" face, or his "that's a tasty-looking finger you have there" face?

We made our introductions and then the owner explained what she came in for. Sultan's upper beak had become overgrown and she was unable to cut it. Relief. This I could handle. Probably. Maybe. The upper beak would normally be like a hook over the lower one, but this one was clearly too long and would interfere with his ability to eat. Trimming it would be like clipping a toenail and wouldn't hurt either of us.

I leaned in to have a closer look. Sultan leaned away with his eye, still beady, fixed on me. I just had to get the right pair of clippers and be quick and decisive about it, but Sultan looked like he could be equally quick and decisive, perhaps more so. I sat back down and thought for a moment.

The owner was astute. She obviously read my face well enough — dilated pupils, sweaty brow, twitchy upper left eyelid — and said, "Sultan can be a bit nippy, so you might want to get some help because I can't hold him if he decides to get rowdy."

No argument from me. I returned with a nurse wearing a pair of our finest welder's gloves. The nurse was fortunately the "no nonsense" type and quickly took command of the situation. In a deft move, she restrained Sultan's head with her right hand while tucking his body against her with her elbow and supporting him with the other arm. He apparently knew he had met his match and submitted to this indignity without a squawk or a struggle. But he kept staring at me the whole time. I nipped the overgrown tip off of his beak and sighed an inner sigh of relief.

The beak trim had been a success, but I didn't feel any more confident around parrots than before, so I circulated a memo: "Philipp will see any species, except parrots."

The other day the new *National Geographic* arrived in the mail. On the cover was a colourfully befeathered dinosaur. And its facial expression was identical to Sultan's.

PELICAN SURPRISE

I like pelicans. I have always liked them. When I was a child in Saskatoon, a favourite outing was to go to the weir on the South Saskatchewan River and watch the pelicans. They were the largest birds I had even seen, and they seemed very exotic to me, although the definition of exotic is admittedly broad when you grow up on the Canadian Prairies. I was a history buff too and they reminded me of those Catalina flying boats of the 1930s and '40s. Then there was a long period of no pelicans in my life until we bought our house here in Winnipeg on the Assiniboine River. There are many wonderful things about this house and property, and one of them is pelicans. We're on a stretch of the river where it's shallow and flows quickly, churning around rocks. The pelicans will float down, scooping up fish, until the water slows again, and then they fly back to the start of the rapids. There are usually four or five of them and they coordinate their fish scoops, dipping and rising in perfect unison. Pelican ballet. This is endlessly fascinating to me.

Imagine my delight then when the zoo phoned to ask whether I would like to ultrasound a pelican. Would I ever! Apparently, they had a graduate student in wildlife veterinary medicine at the zoo who was doing a research project with pelicans. I don't recall what the study was or what specifically the student wanted me to find with the ultrasound, but it doesn't matter for the purposes of this story.

Birds are tricky to ultrasound. Ultrasound is tuned to pass through soft tissues and is blocked by anything considerably more dense, such as bone, or anything considerably less dense, such as air. This is why we put gel on the skin first — to fill any tiny air pockets between the probe and the patient. Birds therefore present two challenges to the ultrasonographer. Not only do they have a massive and inconveniently placed breastbone, but they also have a series of internal air sacs connected to their lungs. These act as bellows to move air much more rapidly through their lungs than we can, improving their ability to absorb oxygen. I'm sure they need all the oxygen they can get. It must be exhausting to flap those wings. Consequently, my window for a pelican ultrasound is much smaller than for a mammal or reptile. The only place to get a clear view is in the middle of the lower abdomen, behind the breastbone and between the air sacs.

The pelican was impressive. I had never seen one up close before. It was a male about a metre and a half long (four and a half feet) and had close to a three-metre wingspan (nine feet), yet he weighed only as much as an average house cat. His feathers were a pristine snowy white with a bright yellow patch around his eyes. His signature massive bill was a similar shade of yellow. He didn't have a name, but in my mind, I called him Gus. What can I say? He just looked like a Gus.

Gus was clearly aggrieved at the indignity of having his daily routine disrupted to be hauled into a strange place. You could see it in his eyes. Consequently, I was surprised that they did not feel the need to sedate him. One of the zoo's vet techs was able to keep Gus still by means of a clever hold. I wasn't sure how much damage he could do with his bill or wings, but I was pleased not to have to find out the hard way.

The grad student and I gingerly plucked a few feathers from his belly. This produced more glares from the disgruntled pelican, but otherwise he didn't react. This was going to be cool. My first ever pelican ultrasound!

White fuzz.

I adjusted the settings and squirted some more gel onto Gus's skin.

Still just white fuzz.

Some of you might be chuckling and saying to yourself, isn't that what ultrasound always looks like? Ha ha. No, it doesn't. Normally there's grey fuzz too. And some black stuff. Here I'm talking about a uniform bright white fuzz across the entire screen.

More adjustments to the settings and some nervous laughter on my part. I was supposed to be the ultrasound expert after all. I had unwisely bragged about being able to ultrasound any animal. Why wasn't the darned thing working?

Then I noticed something odd. There was a crinkling sensation when I applied more pressure with the probe. It reminded me of a dog with subcutaneous emphysema, which is when air gets under the skin because of a tear in the lungs.

"This is weird, but it's like he's got air right under his skin. Has he been injured?" I asked the student.

"Oh no, that's normal for pelicans."

"Normal for pelicans?"

"Yes, they have a network of thousands of little subcutaneous air sacs all along their underside. We're not sure why, but it probably helps them float and it may cushion impact when they hit the water hard. You should see these guys land sometimes. Not very elegant!"

"Huh. Okay, well, it's a problem because ultrasound can't penetrate even the smallest amount of air."

She didn't know that and was surprised. I didn't know they had air under their skin and was surprised. Gus didn't know what the heck was going on and was presumably continuously surprised.

So that was the end of that. The student shrugged and decided that the ultrasound was optional anyway. This was good news for Gus, who was beginning to struggle. I think it's safe to assume that nobody likes to have their air sacs crinkled. And for my part, while it would have been fun to view a pelican's insides, it's more fun to view them on the river, fishing and doing ballet.

THE RATS WHO LOVE CATS

Over the years I've developed a mental checklist of specific diseases to discuss with specific kinds of clients. With campers and hikers, I make sure to talk about Lyme disease. With people who go to Lake of the Woods, I try to remember to talk about blastomycosis (a fungal disease common in the soil there). With people who go to the American Southwest, I talk about Valley Fever (another soil fungus). And with pregnant women, I talk about toxoplasmosis.

Most pregnant women already know they shouldn't scoop the kitty litter because of "something" that might be in the cat's poop but are sometimes hazy on the details of that "something." It turns out that those details are very cool and weird and are, I think, worth spending a little time on.

First, your cat's poop is not a significant source of risk, unless he's a big hunter of rodents. Gardening without gloves is a much bigger risk. This is because stray cats that live on wild rodents are more likely to carry *Toxoplasma gondii* and, as every gardener knows, there's nothing so tempting for a cat to poop in as a patch of freshly turned garden soil. Eating unwashed vegetables is consequently also a risk, as is eating undercooked meat for reasons I will outline below.

Toxo is a wily little organism. It is a single-celled parasitic protozoan, and as such has more in common with amoebas than with bacteria or viruses. Its preferred host is the cat, the only animal it can sexually reproduce in, but it can get into any warm-blooded animal. Consequently, a lot of different life cycles can be mapped out, but let's focus on the one that's relevant to this story, the one that circles between rodents and cats, with occasional regrettable detours to humans. Let's start with what we already know, and that's that Toxo can be spread in cat feces. When a rodent is exposed to these feces by nibbling on contaminated plants or seeds, for example, the Toxo will go into the rodent's tissue. A cat eating this rodent will pick up the Toxo, which will then migrate to the cat's gut, reproduce, and come back out in the feces, thus completing this charming little circle of life. I have oversimplified things greatly, but it's all you need to know for the purposes of what I'm going to tell you next. Incidentally, before I go on, if cattle or pigs are exposed to cat feces, then they become the rodent in this cycle, which is why it can be transmitted in undercooked meat.

Toxo primarily goes into the muscle tissue of these so-called intermediate hosts (mice, rats, gophers, cows, pigs, people, etc.), but it's not picky and it can also choose to go elsewhere. For example, in humans, it can go to the fetus, hence the concerns during pregnancy because during some stages of development fetuses are vulnerable to being damaged by the Toxo. Another favourite alternative destination is the brain, and this is where we get into the cool and weird stuff.

Rats infected with Toxo have been shown to be less afraid of cats. Read that over again and think about it. Before getting this parasite, the rats have a normal, healthy fear of cats, and after they are noticeably less afraid. Not only less afraid, but in many cases, actually *attracted* to cats. Specifically, cat urine, which used to repel them, now excites a sexual response instead. Nothing else changes in their behaviour, only this new-found interest in interspecies love. How can we possibly explain this? The prevailing theory is that Toxo gets into the rats' brains and changes their behaviour to increase the chances of being passed on to their favourite host, the cat. Picture these amoeba-like creatures pulling the strings like tiny puppeteers inside a rat's skull, pulling up the corners of his mouth into a winning rat smile, and then making him lumber awkwardly over to the nearest cat, "Hey baby . . ."

Not weird enough for you? You're in luck. It gets weirder when we involve humans. It turns out that a lot of us have been exposed to Toxo, as up to 30% of the population has antibodies to it. It almost never does any harm. You might have brief flu-like symptoms, but that's about it. This is incidentally also the case with cats. In all my years in practice, I've never diagnosed one as being ill with Toxo. It's not in a clever parasite's interest to damage its host, at least not until it's been manipulated into becoming cat food. Humans are rarely, if ever, eaten by cats, so are we just a boring and pointless host for Toxo? Probably not. Something this pervasive is rarely just random in nature. Or were we once cat food? Did we possibly play the rat role for Toxo with sabre-toothed tigers? If so, is Toxo just hanging around, hoping for large predatory cats to make a comeback? Maybe, but there's another theory why Toxo would evolve to end up in so many of us. Studies indicate that the population with Toxo antibodies has more cats. "Duh!" you say. "That's how we get it, so of course that would be the case." Well, hang on a second. Remember that we hardly ever get Toxo from our own cats. Let me finish. Some scientists believe that the cause-and-effect relationship is the other way around. They see evidence that people who have already been exposed to Toxo (gardening, dirty vegetable eating, raw meat eating) are more likely to subsequently get cats. It's like Toxo is using humans to make cats more popular. That should be weird enough for you.

But I don't go into all that detail with my pregnant clients. I just tell them to wear gloves when they're gardening, in addition to getting someone else to scoop the box. And I tell them to keep loving their cats. It's natural and healthy to do so. We don't need some wacky little amoeba to tell us to do that.

SAUSAGE

My life keeps intersecting with sausage. Does yours too? Maybe it's just me. As a veterinarian and someone who was born in Germany, I suppose my odds are higher.

My earliest clear sausage memory involves my younger brother. He was born in Canada and his German was much more limited. My grandparents always sent us a large Christmas parcel, but often struggled to decide on a gift for him. This was in part because they had difficulty communicating with him when we were in Germany for a visit, and in part because he was an unusual little boy who seemed to be in a world of his own. The parcels came by sea mail and were often weeks late, but we didn't mind as that gave us a second Christmas. Because of this, the anticipation mounted as it only can when little children are given broad leeway to speculate on gifts. We really had no idea. When it finally arrived, we had to wait until my father came home from work before we could open it. We pulsated with excitement all day, no doubt doing violence to my mother's nerves. As soon as my father got home, we tore into the parcel. I opened my gift first. It was a lovely hardcover book. Not at the high end of our speculations, but for a mad reader like me, certainly in the solid middle. Then it was Daniel's turn. My father had his Pentax Spotmatic at the ready to capture the moment of delight so it could be shared with my grandparents. The gift was curiously cylindrical. And it had an indescribable odour that we recognized but couldn't quite place.

Yes, you are correct. Inexplicably, they had sent my brother a sausage. But that's not the best part. The best part is that this sausage had been at sea for six weeks. It was now green and furry. I do not believe there was a more shattered-looking child in all of Saskatoon that Christmas. Possibly not in all the Canadian Prairies. My grandparents were smart and educated people, so this was baffling. Hilarious in retrospect, but baffling.

But it was true, Daniel did love sausage, when it wasn't mouldy, or considered an exciting Christmas gift. We all did. It's a German thing, much more so than sauerkraut, which we never had. We had some form of sausage daily, including taking cans of cocktail wieners on camping trips. Jump ahead a decade and a half and I'm cooking for the first time for my new girlfriend, and future wife. I made "polka dot soup." The polka dots were slices of sausage (wiener specifically). I don't think any further description is required. I am a much better cook now.

I continued to enjoy sausages until that fateful visit to the slaughterhouse one summer when I was collecting pig ovaries for the research lab I worked in. On that visit they decided to show me "The Wiener Machine."

Oh. My. God.

There is so much to say about The Wiener Machine. In fact, I had planned a story for this collection entitled "An Instructive Visit to The Wiener Machine," but decided that was a step too far, even for me. Imagine if Willy Wonka were into pork instead of chocolate, and the Oompa-Loompas were ex-cons, and you've got a good start. That being said, meat inspection and food safety work is a surprisingly common career path for veterinarians, so it would have been a legitimate subject for a book that is ostensibly about the experience of being a veterinarian (more so than mouldly Christmas sausage stories), but I suspect that you really would rather not know how a sausage is made.

But enough about sausage and me. This was all to set you up for Marv Hampton. I've been eating a lot less sausage myself these days, so when I think of sausage now, I think of Marv.

I had just given Ian bad news about Marv. I had discovered a bleeding cancer in the old yellow Lab.

"So, it's best to let him go, is it, Philipp?" Ian Hampton was an elderly Englishman I had known for many years. He had a grey walrus moustache and always wore a flat cap. Margaret had died a few years ago, so it was just Ian and Marv. All euthanasias are hard, but, as mentioned in another story, I am always especially shaken by having to help elderly widows and widowers say goodbye to their last pet. Even writing this is hard.

"Yes, I'm afraid so. We could consider surgery, but at his age and given the fact that it's probably spread, I don't recommend it. I'm so very sorry."

"Can I take him home for one night? I'll bring him back tomorrow."

"Yes, of course. He's not really suffering right now."

"I'm going to give him his favourite sausage. You told me to stop years ago, but I figure it's okay now."

Yes, that was right. Now I remembered. The Hamptons loved their English breakfast sausages — "proper bangers" — and had gradually increased the amount they gave Marv, as he sat patiently staring at them every morning. Eventually Marv himself began to resemble a giant sausage. I gave them the predictable diet advice, not really expecting much to change, but on the next annual visit he had slimmed down substantially. They told me Marv seemed satisfied with a crust of toast instead. I always doubted they really believed that, but I admired their fortitude and perseverance. The sausage-free Marv went on to live a long, healthy life.

"Please do! Give him the juiciest sausage with my compliments."

We both chuckled, but we were both holding back tears. Marv, however, looked more alert than he had in days. I suspect he remembered the word.

SCREAMING BEAGLES

We are in the midst of the Beagle Revival, or, if you prefer, the Second Great Age of the Beagle. The First Great Age of the Beagle followed Snoopy's appearance in the Peanuts cartoon strip in 1950. Snoopy's resemblance to a real beagle was iffy, but he was a cultural phenomenon that produced a halo effect for his alleged breed. Beagles, along with cocker spaniels and German shepherds, ruled for a couple decades, but breed popularity can be subject to fashion, and by the 1970s beagles were no longer cool. Nor was Snoopy, for that matter. (An aside regarding how long ago this really was: my spell-checker wants me to write Snoop, not Snoopy.) But now they're back. After seeing maybe one beagle puppy every two or three years, I'm now seeing them every other month or so. Them and dachshunds and French bulldogs. I don't want to overstate things, because Labs, golden retrievers, poodles, chihuahuas, and shih tzus are still far more popular, but they have always been popular, so it's not a fair comparison.

I like beagles. They're smart* and they're funny and they have buckets of personality. But if I were to offer a critique, I would say they can be too loud. The baying of a beagle is a distinctive sound. It brings a fox hunt to mind. I'm sure it's quite evocative for some people, although I must say that I agree with Oscar Wilde, who called fox hunting "the unspeakable in pursuit of the uneatable." But baying is just part of a beagle's repertoire. They also bark and yip and howl. And they scream. I'm not sure any other dog screams the way a beagle does. Consider yourself lucky if you haven't heard a beagle scream. It is a heartrending sound and in a busy and chaotic clinic, it can be the one extra ingredient that turns the day into a real-life Anacin commercial.

Julius was a cool beagle. He was cool like the Snoopy of old. He was always happy to see me, and his owners often had wacky stories to tell of the hijinks he had gotten up to. On the day in question, though, they weren't with him because of the pandemic lockdown. He had been dropped

---

* This is an unpopular opinion. According to one researcher, beagles ranked 131st out of 138 breeds for intelligence. But that has not been my experience. Because many breeds are so specialized in what they were originally bred for, standard dog intelligence tests can be unfair. Get a beagle on the hunt for a speck of food you've hidden somewhere and then see how dumb you think he is. Also, most dog intelligence tests are inadvertently also testing for obedience. Stubbornness is not the same thing as stupidity, although it may seem that way sometimes, both with dogs and, it must be said, people.

off with the history that he seemed to be in pain, and they didn't know why. I approached his kennel, looking forward to seeing him. As soon as I crouched down and reached to open the door he began to scream. I immediately pulled my hand back.

He screamed so loud that someone yelled from the adjacent treatment room, "Oh my God, Philipp, what are you doing to that poor dog?!"

"I haven't even touched him yet!"

I stood up and stepped back. He stopped screaming.

I waited a moment, and then tried again. He screamed again. If anything, even louder.

Staff began to gather. Shocked looks were exchanged. I can only imagine what the other dogs in the clinic were thinking, "I knew it! My humans said it was going to be okay, but it's not! It is so totally not okay!"

What to do?

I would just have to bite the bullet and scoop the poor dog out. I knew Julius well enough to be confident he wouldn't bite me, but I feared for the health of my eardrums. Seriously. And I felt terrible for him, but the only way to make him better was to first figure out what was wrong. I had my suspicions, but I still needed to examine him. Beagles may be the dramatic divas of the dog world, but this screaming was beyond that. I had no doubt that he was in pain.

It's actually called "Beagle Pain Syndrome." Well, it's not called that anymore, but that's the name I was taught and it's much easier to remember than the modern, more technically precise term, "Steroid-Responsive Meningitis-Arteritis," or SRMA. It may be more precise, but whenever a disease name includes the treatment, you can bet there's not enough known about the cause, otherwise that would be in the name instead. Because it responds to steroids, most researchers assume it's an autoimmune condition, but nobody's willing to call it "Immune-Mediated Meningitis-Arteritis" yet. SRMA affects other breeds too, such as Nova Scotia duck tollers (incidentally, my vote for coolest breed name) and border collies, but beagles are the poster children.

This is what Julius had. I had to put a muzzle on the unfortunate dog to allow myself to think and talk to my colleagues and staff. He had such sad eyes when I put the muzzle on that I wanted to hug him, but that would make the pain and screaming, albeit now stifled, even worse, so I limited myself to trying to soothe him with words. This was a complete failure. It reminded me of when I was trying to soothe Lorraine with words when she was in labour.

I localized the pain to the part of the spine in his neck, the rest of his exam was normal, his bloodwork was normal, and x-rays of the area were normal. Beagle Pain Syndrome is a diagnosis of exclusion unless you want to do a spinal tap. I had ruled out the other common possibilities, and a spinal tap is tricky to get right and tricky to analyze properly. Moreover, this was very much a "walks like a duck, talks like a duck" scenario. We can sometimes waste a lot of time (not to mention the client's money) trying to guarantee the accuracy of our diagnoses. Knowing when to stop testing and start treating is, I suppose, an art.

I called Julius's people and proposed that we try him on a course of steroids. They agreed and I am delighted to report that within a few days he was back to himself. No more screaming. Only baying, and for once, the baying was a relief.

SCRUMPY

I expect that most of you reading this assume that Scrumpy refers to a cute name for a pet, perhaps a scruffy little terrier or a cool long-haired orange tomcat. But a small number of you are thinking something else. Those of you are correct. And that something else is the punchline to this story, so if you are one of those clever folks, read on with a satisfied smile. The rest of you can enjoy the mystery of wondering what on earth I'm talking about.

Scout was a black Lab–border collie cross, who, for a time, might have been the most charming dog in the practice. He was always eager to come in and would sit patiently for his examinations and treatments. He knew exactly when to offer his paw for shaking, and he always cocked his head to one side when you spoke to him. I don't think I ever saw him without his big doggie smile, at least not until that day in late September when he came in sicker than he had ever been before.

It was a stunning autumn afternoon and I'll confess I was feeling mildly annoyed at being at work. I would so much rather have been out walking in the woods. Peak leaf colour only lasts about a week or two in Manitoba, and it is a rare treat for that to coincide with good weather and with a day off. I was going to miss it by one day, as I was off the next day and rain was forecast. Oh well. As a consolation, I was going to see Scout. I was pleased about that, at least until I realized how sick he was.

He was unable to walk in on his own, so the staff carried him to the exam room on a stretcher.

"He can't walk, and he's not eating either," Mrs. Stevens said. She was a tall, elderly woman who had been coming to the practice for decades. There was a Mr. Stevens as well, a small, almost gnomic man, but he almost always stayed in the car, so I seldom saw him. And when he came in, he never said anything, but just sat in the corner and grinned. Today he stayed in the car.

"When did this start?" I asked.

"Suddenly this morning. He was right as rain yesterday."

"Did he have any different food or treats? Or any way he could have had an accident without you noticing?"

"No, everything was normal, and we keep a close eye on him. He goes in the yard on his own, but there's nothing there that could hurt him. There's just the patio furniture, my vegetable garden, a couple apple trees, and a locked toolshed."

I greeted Scout and offered him a liver treat. He refused it, looking mournful with his lower eyelids sagging and famous smile absent.

"Okay, buddy, I'm going to help you stand up," I said softly as I put an arm under Scout's midsection and slowly hoisted him into a standing position. He swayed slightly as I let go and then slid his feet to the side to brace himself. He hung his head low, looking doleful and pathetic.

"Oh, my poor Scouty!" Mrs. Stevens said.

I was suspicious that some sort of central nervous system disorder had befallen him, so, crouched by his side, I carefully went through all his reflexes, but they were normal. The rest of the examination was normal as well, other than the obvious facts that he was weak, wobbly, and depressed. I tried to get him to walk a few steps, but he stumbled and almost fell over.

"That's what he's been like all morning! What do you think, Dr. Schott?"

I eased Scout back down into a more comfortable lying position and rocked back on my heels as I briefly pondered my answer.

"I honestly don't know. His vitals are good, and there are no obvious signs of trauma or major internal problems like bleeding."

"Will you run some tests then?"

"Yes, that's the best next step. We'll pull some blood and see what that shows us. I'd like to keep him for a few hours for observation as well if that's okay." I had the feeling I was missing something obvious and hoped buying some time would help reveal the something. Scout reminded me of something or someone, but I couldn't quite put my finger on it.

I made myself a nuisance in the lab area as I waited impatiently for the blood results. I had convinced myself that his weakness was because of a potassium deficiency, although I hadn't yet ridden that train of thought far enough to come up with a sensible theory as to why Scout would suddenly develop that.

I didn't have to because his potassium was normal. In fact, all his bloodwork was normal. Even though I had ruled a few things out, I didn't feel like I was any further ahead. Ruling things out is most helpful when there's a concrete list of possibilities that you have made shorter with your rule-outs. But in the absence of such a list, it felt more like shouting random names into a large crowd in the hopes that the person might be there and answer.

"Let's get some urine," I told one of the techs, in another blind stab at trying to find useful data.

"Can I walk him outside?" she asked, looking doubtfully at the recumbent dog.

"If you get some help, you can probably sling-walk him." Sling-walking is where you put a towel under the midsection of a dog to support their weight.

She got another tech to help her and with some effort they got Scout slowly walking down the hall towards the back door. He swayed and stumbled, but with the two of them helping, they were able to keep him upright.

"He looks drunk, Philipp!"

Drunk.

That was what he reminded me of. I had seen a patient stoned after accidental marijuana ingestion a few months prior. That dog also had dilated pupils and was sleepy, but intoxication of some kind fit the symptoms perfectly. It fit the symptoms, but it didn't fit the history. This was before marijuana legalization here, and the Stevens struck me as the rigorously law-abiding types, although I suppose you never can be certain. And in any case, the tech was right: this looked more like drunkenness. But how would a dog get into alcohol?

It was time for an awkward phone call.

"So, the good news is that Scout's blood tests came back normal, meaning that major organ function is good. Of course, this also means we don't have a diagnosis yet, but in watching him try to walk, I have a suspicion." I paused and took a deep breath. "This might sound strange, but is there any chance that Scout could somehow get access to alcohol?"

"Alcohol? I can hardly imagine how. We always keep the liquor cabinet closed!" she laughed.

"I know it sounds like a silly question, but he does look intoxicated."

We agreed that he would be kept longer for observation and I hung up, feeling foolish.

Then suddenly, as I was walking back to the treatment area to have another look at Scout, I had one of those rare but very welcome flashes of insight. I turned around and called her back immediately.

"I thought of something else. Those apple trees you mentioned before — are there very many apples on the ground?"

"Hardly any. Scout always cleans them up! There were lots this year, so it took him longer because we stopped him from eating too many at once so he wouldn't get sick."

That was it. The apples left lying longer until Scout was allowed to eat them had fermented. Wild fermented apple juice produces a cider called "scrumpy" in the English west country. If you have the taste for it, it's a delicious treat. Scout evidently had the taste for it, but what he didn't have was alcohol dehydrogenase. That's the enzyme our ancestors developed as a mutation when we were still covered in hair and living in the African bush. It allowed them to metabolize alcohol so they could safely eat the fermented fruit lying on the forest floor. It would give them a buzz, but the nutritional value was the main benefit. Only humans, chimps, and gorillas have alcohol dehydrogenase. Dogs do not, so dogs get much drunker much faster on small amounts of alcohol.

It took the whole day, but by evening Scout was able to walk a straight line again. He even got his doggie smile back.

I expect Scout probably developed a nasty hangover, but that wouldn't teach him not to eat scrumpy apples again as he wouldn't make the connection. Heck, it's not even enough to teach humans, and we don't have that excuse.

SKIN AND BONES

Night was a new patient who had been dropped off for assessment for whenever I had time as no scheduled appointments were available. All that was noted was Night's species (feline), his gender (neutered male), and his owner's name, address, and phone number. There was no age given and the only history offered by the owner on dropping him off was "just skin and bones, but eats good."

One of my appointments finished early and the next client called to say they were running late, so I suddenly had a spare moment. I went back into the wards to look for Night. It was a busy day, so almost every cage was occupied with the usual array of dogs and cats, some quiet and some loud, some shy and some outgoing, some quite ill and some seemingly in perfect health. Night's cage was the last one. At first, I didn't see him because he was in a dark back corner, curled up, and, as his name implied, he was black, jet black. I opened the cage and spoke to him softly. There was no response. He still lay there in a tight curl, not moving.

Was he even breathing? I felt a flutter of alarm. I had been a couple of hours in getting to him, but nobody had indicated that it was an emergency.

Oh no, is he DIC?

DIC is the most dreaded acronym in veterinary medicine. Technically, it stands for "disseminated intravascular coagulation," a fatal disturbance of the body's clotting mechanism, but commonly it's also used for "dead in cage." Please don't let Night be DIC. I haven't even spoken to his people yet.

I reached in carefully and touched him on the side of his chest.

It was moving.

And he stirred.

He opened his eyes, lifted his head slightly, yawned, and stretched all four legs out so far that it seemed they were made of rubber. Then, ever so slowly, he got to his feet, wobbly like a newborn calf. He gave himself a shake and almost fell over. I have seen a lot of skinny cats over the years, probably thousands who were too thin, and among them hundreds who qualified as truly emaciated. Night was a step or two beyond emaciated. I couldn't remember ever seeing a thinner cat. Skin and bones indeed.

He may have been mostly skin and bones, but fortunately his purring motor was still there too, and it made him practically rattle as I examined him. Staff walking by would invariably comment, "Oh my god, that cat's so skinny!" Yes, I know. On examination he had a fast heart rate, a fast respiratory rate, and a large thyroid gland. Otherwise, he was in remarkably good shape, given his lack of fat or muscle. The diagnosis was obvious. I was sure he had an overactive thyroid gland, although there could be other conditions complicating this. I estimated him to be 12-ish years old, but it was time to find out for sure and get some more information about Night, so I called the owners.

The phone call was not especially productive. I learned that Night was "at least ten years old," but he had been the owner's son's cat, and he had moved away, so she wasn't sure. She reported no other symptoms, just the obvious extreme skinniness, and the paradoxical excellent appetite. Apparently, this had been going on for a while, but again she wasn't sure because since her son's departure over six months ago she didn't see much of Night or interact with him other than to put food down. I worried that this meant she wouldn't be willing to run any tests or treat anything, but she gave me the green light to do whatever needed to be done to help the skinny old boy.

I told the tech to go ahead and get a blood sample to check his thyroid level, as well as a general blood chemistry panel to make sure everything else was functioning well. I still had a few minutes before my next appointment, so I went back into the office. I was staring morosely at the list of phone messages and emails, trying to decide what order to tackle them in, when an assistant came running in.

"They need you in the back, Philipp! There's a problem with that skinny cat."

I sprinted into the treatment room and saw that Night was lying on his side, gasping.

"He started to do this as soon as we got him into position for the blood draw!"

I snatched a stethoscope off the table and had a careful listen. His heart rate was even faster than before, and a little erratic now. His lungs sounded clear, though. Hyperthyroid cats always have fast hearts, but in combination with the distressed breathing, it made me wonder whether he was also going into heart failure. In extreme cases, high levels of thyroid hormone can cause the heart muscle to thicken to the point that it causes problems. I had only seen that a couple of times in my 30 years in practice as we usually catch hyperthyroidism earlier. Also, this condition fills the space between the lungs and chest wall with fluid, muffling the heart, but Night's heart sounds were clear. I was confused.

Night was beginning to turn blue.

"Let's take him into ultrasound," I said as I trotted ahead to set the machine up.

Heart failure patients can be extremely fragile, like that proverbial house of cards. Everything can seem okay, and then the slightest stress can cause a collapse and death, sometimes in seconds. Consequently, we moved him as gently as possible into the darkened ultrasound room and kept the handling to a bare minimum.

The screen lit up. There was the heart — yes, the walls were far too thick — and there was the fluid in the space around the lungs. Yet it hadn't muffled the sound as it normally did. That just goes to show that for every rule in medicine, there is an exception.

I was focused on the ultrasound screen, so I asked, "How's his breathing?"

"He's not gasping at the moment, but it's still really laboured and his colour isn't good."

There was no time to phone Night's owner, so I hoped the green light she gave me still applied.

"I'm going to grab the pleurocentesis set-up."

Pleurocentesis is the process whereby you draw fluid out of the chest cavity through a needle and syringe. Night was going to drown internally if I didn't try.

He didn't flinch as I inserted the long needle between his ribs, using the ultrasound to guide it so that I wouldn't accidentally hit the heart.

50 millilitres, then 100, then 150, then 200, then 250 millilitres. I pulled a full cup of pale straw-coloured fluid out of his chest cavity. Nobody said anything during this procedure, and it seemed like nobody breathed either.

"How is he?" I asked as I pulled the needle out and exhaled.

The tech was quiet for a moment. "Good. He's good," she said with obvious relief.

I turned on the light just as she let Night go. He stretched his rubbery stretch again, stood up, and looked around. His breathing was much better.

Minutes later he was chowing down on a big bowl of cat food and acting in every way like he hadn't just been knocking on death's door. Imagine if you had just had a big needle in your chest pulling out the human equivalent of a gallon of fluid. Would your first thought afterwards be "Lunchtime!"?

I imagine not. Cats are amazing creatures.

His bloodwork confirmed the hyperthyroidism. With even just a small amount of luck, successful treatment will reverse his heart changes, help him put on some weight, and allow him to go and live a normal life. My impression is that Night and luck have an excellent working relationship.

SMELLY PANTS

Thank you for making it past the title. In truth, it is the mildest and least offensive title I could come up with for what follows. Consider yourself amply forewarned, or, depending on your personal tastes and predilections, amply teased.

There are many basic truths about veterinary medicine. Most of them are too self-evident to bother listing off. If you're reading this book I'm sure you've got a handle on the common joys and challenges we face, but one challenge I haven't spent too much time on is the grossness of a lot of what we do. Sure, I've hinted at it here and there, and in a previous book I joked about how a veterinarian is either the most entertaining or the most appalling dinner guest you can imagine — or both — because we all have cartloads of gross-out stories that we love to share. But it's tricky, isn't it? Almost everyone enjoys a funny story, or a sad story, or a cute story, but only some people enjoy a gross story. I suppose they're versions of horror stories, and horror is easily the most polarizing genre in writing and film. As you can imagine, after over 30 years in practice I have a lot of these stories, but in deference to my more sensitive readers, I've decided to compact them all into this one story, the story of my smelly pants.

Much of the grossness of veterinary medicine revolves around the various substances animals emit when they're ill, or frightened, or just in the mood. It's a subject of some debate within the profession as to which substance is the worst to get on you, and what part of you is the worst for it to land on. Veterinarians quickly learn to keep their mouths closed when there is even the slightest risk, so by general agreement, that's not on the list of options. And the blink reflex is gratifyingly efficient, so eyes are very improbable too. Consequently, as far as I'm concerned, it's hair. Hair is the worst place for a gross substance to land, but it happens.

I'm going to check in before I continue. Are you still with me? Ready to forge on? Good.

So, given that I think hair is the worst, I am fortunate. I've never gotten anything in my hair other than a little blood, but one of my colleagues got anal sac secretions into hers. That was bad. Sometimes when you express the sacs, the stuff jets out under high pressure. We once painted the blinds in Room Five with it. Not a week goes by where I don't have to change my lab coat because of it. But into your hair? Yuck. Even I would find that gross.

She washed her hair in the sink after, yelling "Ew! Ew! Ew!" the whole time.

But I've had just about every other substance just about everywhere else. I've had gooey cat vomit on my shoes, bloody puppy diarrhea on my hands, nasty cat abscess pus on my sleeves, smelly dog pee on my pants (more on that in a moment), and, memorably, gory blood from a big dog surgery across my face. There was an arterial spurt, and it painted a perfect vertical line right across my gown, mask, upper face, and surgical cap. The bleeding was easily controlled, so the getting blood on me is by itself not memorable. No, what was memorable is that I forgot to wash my face before going into an appointment (Please see the earlier story "The Lapse" for an avowal of absent-mindedness). I had taken my gown, mask, and cap off, and I had washed my hands, but I hadn't thought about my face. The client kept staring at me in a peculiar way but didn't say anything. I hadn't met them before, so I thought that perhaps they were trying to place my face from somewhere else, like maybe our kids attended the same school. But they seemed curiously in a hurry to finish up the visit and leave, so it couldn't be that. Oh well, some people are strange. Then the receptionist suggested I look in the mirror.

Now on to the smelly pants. Orbit, my dog, loves it when I come home from work. I presume he loves to have me home, but he also loves to give my pants a thorough sniff when I've been at the clinic. Every now and again it's a bonus day for him because I've gotten one of the aforementioned substances on my pants. Oh, how deeply he sniffs them then, his nostrils flaring, his tail slowly wagging like a hairy metronome. But the return home that must stand out for Orbit was the day I got hosed down by Frank.

Frank was an unneutered 60-kilogram (135-pound) male crossbred dog. I don't recall why he came in, but I will never forget what happened when I finished the exam and stood up to talk to his owner. Frank was at my side. He was quiet and, as far as I knew, not doing anything other than just standing there waiting for the humans to conclude their mysterious business. Then the side of my leg began to feel warm and wet. At first just a little, then a lot. This was such a strange and unexpected sensation that I didn't immediately react, thinking my senses were fooling me. There was no sound, no smell (not yet anyway — that came soon, though), and nothing to see as I wasn't facing that way. Just suddenly warm and wet. Weird.

Frank's owner, a big-bellied man with a lumberjack beard, burst out laughing, "Ha ha, Doc! He's so pissed off at you that he's pissed on you!"

I whirled around and, sure enough, the outside of my right pant leg was sopping wet. The pee was beginning to drip into my shoes. Frank looked at me with a bored facial expression, as if to say, "Yeah, so what? I needed to pee, and your leg was nearest vertical object."

Frank's owner was almost beside himself with mirth. He did apologize, although it was between repeats of his too-clever "pissed off/pissed on" turn of phrase.

I don't keep a change of pants at work (why would I?), and the surgical scrub pants we keep in reserve were too small, so I just sponged the urine off with paper towel and gave my pant leg a quick scrub, knowing that it was going to be a banner day for Orbit when I got home. While I did so, I had a flashback to my childhood. I was ten years old and at the Saskatoon Forestry Farm Park Zoo on a sparkling clear January day. Oddly enough, among all the usual Canadian suspects — bears, caribou, elk, wolves — there was an African lion. He was a gorgeous animal, his fur all the more luxuriant because of the Prairie winter. As a little boy I was especially fascinated by the sign on his enclosure that stated, "Caution: I'm a cat, so I spray backwards!" This was helpfully accompanied by a cartoon lion doing exactly that through the bars. I have a vivid visual memory of the day in question. I was standing about 20 small-boy paces to the west of the cage, while a well-dressed woman was right up against the north side of the cage, captivated by the lion as he paced in a large circle and roared. Then he swung his back end towards her and, without warning, let loose an astonishing torrent of urine, drenching the woman. She was steaming, literally steaming, as the warm pee hit her cold jacket. She was too stunned to make a sound. It was one of the top three most amazing things I had seen in my life to that point. I couldn't wait to tell my friends.

But back to Winnipeg in the present day.

So, that was gross. Frank's deluge wasn't nearly the same volume, nor did it steam, but it was still gross. For those of you thinking of going into veterinary medicine, but now a little bit frightened, I can tell you that you get used to it. You really do. And for my money, human medicine is so much worse. I can write about all the things in this story with a smile on my face and a song in my heart, but if I even begin to think about some of the grimmer aspects of human medicine, I feel so squeamish that I have to change the channel in my head. Even something as banal as having to look between people's toes. Nope, nope, nope. But give me a juicy cat abscess that's getting ready to burst . . .

SOLVITUR AMBULANDO

Solvitur ambulando: "It is solved by walking." I have a lot of favourite quotes, but this is my most favourite one. I might even consider having it inscribed on my tombstone, if only for the enjoyment of the irony.

However, while alive, *it is* solved by walking. Which "it" am I referring to? Really any problem I have been thinking about, whether in my personal life, my writing, or my veterinary practice. Some people think these things over in the bath, or with a cup of tea, or while out gardening, golfing, or running, but I prefer to walk. I won't bore (or alarm) you with any details regarding the personal problems, but the connection to writing is very straightforward. On a writing day I will alternate walks with bouts of typing. I can only two-finger type and stare at a glowing screen for so long before my brain begins to feel like day-old oatmeal. A walk reliably refreshes and resets, and moreover, when I am stuck on some aspect of what I am writing, the solution frequently presents itself over the course of the walk. This very story wrote itself in my head while I was meandering through the forest with Orbit, admiring the busy woodpeckers.

The link to veterinary problem solving is perhaps less obvious, but it works the same way. Towards the end of a shift my brain will also have evolved to an amorphous gooey state wherein useful thoughts can only be extracted from it with painful effort. There's only so much input that poor little organ can accommodate before it begins to struggle. Fortunately, a lot of what we do is rote. For example, I'm sure I could fill a syringe with rabies vaccine while blindfolded and yodelling "Oh! Susanna." Not that I have ever needed to do so, but should that need arise, I'm your man. I'm sure of it. And a lot of other things can be stalled. This is the classic "take two aspirins and call me in the morning" scenario. Sometimes this is perfectly valid and useful advice (although never two aspirins with our pets), but sometimes it's just a stalling tactic because our gloopy brains need time to process additional information before making important decisions. That night, after work, I'll go for a walk, and often finish it feeling much clearer about what was baffling me. I may still be baffled, but at least

I'll have greater clarity about the nature of the bafflement, which is a useful start.

But if it's not rote, and I cannot stall, and my brain is cooked, then oh, how I would love to be able to take a short walk. Obviously, this is almost impossible during the workday, so sometimes sitting quietly at my desk for a few deep breaths or, better yet, in the bathroom for 60 seconds of alone time will have to do. And somehow, I manage, and somehow, reasonably good decisions still mostly get made. But a walk would be better.

Let me back up a little. I wrote that walks are almost impossible during the workday. That's not the same thing as totally impossible. Once in a proverbial blue moon I will be blessed with a lunch break long enough to permit a walk, and when it happens on one of those brain porridge days, it feels like the gods are smiling on me. If I only have 15 minutes, I'll go around the block, but if I have half an hour or more and have my car with me (I often walk or cycle to work), then I'll drive to the Assiniboine Forest, just five minutes from the clinic.

This happened the other day when I was struggling with a case. Penny was a beautiful black labradoodle who had come in with a history of "ADR." ADR is vet-specific acronym for "ain't doin' right." Confusingly, in human medicine it stands for "adverse drug reaction" (which could, I suppose, lead to the veterinary ADR). An ADR patient has vague non-specific symptoms. They often are eating less, are less energetic, and just don't seem like themselves to the owner. There are hundreds of potential causes. Probably thousands. In Penny's case, her ADR symptoms waxed and waned, but the trend was towards steady worsening. Physical exam, blood tests, urine tests, and x-rays all revealed nothing. I even did an ultrasound, squeezed in between two appointments on that busy morning, but it was unremarkable too. According to all that testing, she was healthy, but she so obviously wasn't. Penny was normally a happy patient, keen to meet people, and peppy even in the hospital, but today she wasn't. She moped in her kennel and refused treats.

I had a long lunch break scheduled that day and had somehow managed to catch up enough that I was able to sneak out of the building for a walk in the forest, and hopefully a recharge. I walked by Penny's cage on my way out and tried to coax a wag or even just an eyebrow raise out of her, but no luck.

The approach to problem solving when walking is an indirect one. I briefly think about the issue at the start of the walk, and then let it go and allow my mind to wander at will. I'm sure the neuroscientists have something to say about how this works, something to do with the default mode network in the posterior cingulate, but what I know is that my mind wanders differently when I'm walking. After a few minutes, the jangly racing thoughts settle down and a smoother flow develops. This could be about anything from the weather to the show I watched last night. If I'm unlucky, sometimes it's an earworm — you know, those catchy songs that loop continuously in your brain, unbidden. At least it's never a stressy jumble anymore. Sometimes this is all that happens, smooth but unproductive thoughts. No problems solved, but I feel calmer and readier for what's next. But often some sort of solution will suddenly appear, as if by sleight of hand (sleight of mind?). One second, it's how beautifully the pussy willows glow in the sun or the 11th round of "We are the champions, my friend . . ." and the next second it's Addison's disease. Penny has atypical Addison's disease. Probably. Maybe.

There it was, a solution presenting itself out of the subconscious, scuttling crabwise into view. Staring at the rock where the crab was hiding would have made it nervous, so not thinking about the problem directly was helpful, but there is also something special about walking, at least for me. It seems to relax the crabs even more and give them confidence to show themselves.

A specialized test was needed to confirm atypical Addison's, which is a dysfunction of the adrenal glands. This version is "atypical" because it doesn't disturb the sodium and potassium and is therefore not detected on the routine tests. Penny tested positive and responded well to treatment.

Many of my colleagues participating in the play-along-at-home version probably guessed Addison's several paragraphs ago, but that day I needed to do a Ctrl-Alt-Del on my brain first. I needed to solve it by walking.

THE SONG OF THE GUINEA PIG

I dearly hope that one day I will meet a guinea pig named Pavarotti. To my mind that is the perfect name for this operatic species. Pavarotti would be a dark-coloured tousle-furred Abyssinian guinea pig, with a glint in his eye and a voice that carries all the way to the parking lot. But alas, most of them are named Cuddles (even though very few are actually cuddly) or Bailey (even though that always brings to mind a cocker spaniel or golden retriever). For some reason I like human names, like Priscilla or Frank, for this species more than for any other type of pet. And that's just based on their inherently comical appearance. Add the song of the guinea pig, and you'll see why Pavarotti is perfect, or Bono, or Elvis, or Jay-Z, if you prefer.

No other small pet has the vocal range of the guinea pig. From little contented chirps to eardrum-rending shrieks of terror, these guys have a lot to say. Those little chirps while they're going about their routine happy guinea pig business are charming to listen to. At least I find them charming, but then I don't live with a guinea pig. Some owners report that it does start to wear thin after a while, necessitating Bailey's move to a distant, or more sound-proof, room. I also find these sounds charming because it means my patient is relaxed and not stressed. This is rare with guinea pigs, quite rare. I can't think of another species that so easily and routinely slips into panic mode. I often only need to step into the exam room and Cuddles will dive for shelter and begin squealing at the top of her teensy-tiny lungs like I'm a foul slavering predator preparing to make a meal of her. In this scenario the ratio of pet decibels to pet grams is extraordinary and, given that I avoid seeing parrots, probably the highest of any of my regular patients.

Then three years ago I went to Peru and for the first time observed guinea pigs in their native habitat. There I had a light-bulb moment. A word about the name first, though. Guinea pigs are neither from Guinea, which is in Africa, nor (duh) are they pigs, or even related in any way to pigs. They are native to the Andes mountains in South America and were first brought to England by sailors in the 1500s. Nobody knows for sure, but it's likely they sailed from a port in Guyana, in northern South America, and that was corrupted to Guinea. And the pig part is because the squeals reminded people of the noises piglets make. Or so the story goes. If you own and love a guinea pig, are faint of heart, and can't already guess the next part of this story, then perhaps skip to the end where I describe how cute the babies are. The darker explanation for "pig" is that they are, I'm afraid to say, apparently tasty as well as cute.

Rabbits also occupy this disturbing borderland between pet and food, but the food part is much less common and is kept well hidden in our society. For the guinea pig, however, which side of that divide they sit on depends entirely on where they live. Here, all guinea pigs are pets, and none are eaten. In Peru, all guinea pigs are food, and none are pets. My brother and I were on a hike and were staying in our guide's village. We slept in a relatively modern guesthouse but were invited into the hut of one of his family members for dinner one night. I stooped to step through the low door and immediately set off a storm of squealing as at least a dozen guinea pigs scattered to hide under benches and in dark corners.

Our guide chuckled. "They're used to us and know we've made dinner already, so they're safe from us for today, but when someone they don't know comes in . . ." He made a scattering motion with his hands, squealed a few times, and laughed.

Foul slavering predator indeed. No doubt a deep genetic memory persists.

We were not offered guinea pig that night, nor did we partake when it was offered in various restaurants in the towns. One had a beautiful chalk drawing on its menu board of a smiling guinea pig holding up a platter bearing a charred friend. I suppose it's not that different than the cartoon chickens here exhorting us to eat their brethren. But still it felt different as I don't have any pet chickens as patients. This is a morally dubious distinction to make, I know, but they had drawn that guinea pig with a jaunty little scarf around his neck, like Pavarotti.

I promised you a cute guinea pig baby reference. Here it is. Guinea pigs are unique in that their babies look like miniature adults — same proportions, same coat, same everything, just much smaller. Puppies look puppyish, kittens look kittenish, human babies look babyish — except the unfortunate few who resemble tiny Winston Churchills — but guinea pig pups (no, curiously not piglets) are adorably like the cast of *Honey I Shrunk the Guinea Pig*. Imagine that, and imagine the charming chirps, and forget all the stuff about shrieking and charring so that you can leave this story with a smile.

STRING THEORY

There are few presentations in veterinary medicine that open the door to as many possibilities as the cat who has stopped eating. Give me a dog who is itchy, and I can be confident that it's one of two or three things. Ditto for the cat having trouble peeing, or the dog with diarrhea. But a cat who doesn't want her dinner anymore? There are a hundred causes, and it is rarely simple or quick to figure out. I love cats, and I love solving problems, but I don't love these cases.

However, I can quickly narrow things down with two pieces of information: how old is the kitty, and did this come on suddenly, or has she been gradually losing appetite over a long period of time?

Buttercup was one year old and, according to the note in the appointment booking, she had stopped eating three days ago, so I went into the room assuming that we were most likely dealing with either a viral infection or what we delicately refer to as a "dietary indiscretion." She was a beautiful dark tabby, with the softest fur and brilliant green eyes, and she was the object of adoration by the six-year-old girl who had insisted on hauling the carrier in herself, leaning heavily to the side, both hands clamped on the handle. Her father helped her heft the carrier up onto the exam table, though.

Buttercup was wary of me and squirmed vigorously while I examined her. The little girl, who stood by the exam table and attempted to help hold Buttercup for me, tried to comfort her, saying, "It's okay. Buttercup, the doctor's going to make you better." Buttercup was unconvinced, but I was able to get most of the examination done and had concluded that it probably wasn't a virus. Her temperature was normal, she had no other symptoms, and there was no likely exposure history. No, this was probably going to be something she ate. Her belly was tense, which could just be anxiety, and she was especially reluctant to allow me to look in her mouth, which could also just be anxiety, but I had a theory.

My theory was string.

"Does Buttercup get into anything she shouldn't around the house? Like plants or plastic wrap or rubber bands, or things like string and thread?"

"Yes, she's a very bad kitten. She gets into everything!" the girl said. Her father, who was sitting on a chair in the corner of the room doing something on his phone, nodded emphatically without looking up from the screen.

"A typical kitten then! I'm going to get a nurse to give me a hand because I'd like to take a closer look inside her mouth. I have a sneaking suspicion about what I'm going to see in there."

With the tech's help I was able to get a split-second glance under Buttercup's tongue. Sure enough, I could see a loop of string caught under the tongue. No other species does this, but cats who chew on string or thread routinely get it snagged there, and then swallow both ends. Anchored like that, the string doesn't go anywhere. Sometimes they vomit it back up, but not often enough, and even when they do, they often foolishly just try to swallow it again. Cats are smart in specific ways, but they are also dumb in many other specific ways.

I explained to the girl and her father what I had seen and that the next step would be to sedate Buttercup and then snip the string, so that each end would be free to go down.

"You can't just pull it out?" the father asked.

"No, unfortunately there's too much risk that dragging it back up could damage delicate tissues in the back of the throat or in her digestive tract."

The girl looked worried. "But she's going to be okay, right?"

"This usually works really well." I said this with as confident a tone as I could. I err on the side of the glass being half full, so sometimes I fail to be explicit about how things can go wrong. To be fair, this particular glass was at least three-quarters full — cutting the string usually does work — but there was a chance it could still get caught up somewhere else in the system, especially if there was a knot in the string, or something else attached to it. I had asked them whether they had any idea where the string came from, but the dad had shrugged and said, "With three kids, two cats, and a dog . . . who knows?"

When string doesn't pass, it becomes a big problem. The intestines will keep contracting around the string, trying to get it to move, and in doing so will start to bunch up, like a shirt sleeve being pushed up an arm. In the worst cases the string can become so taut that it begins to saw through the loops of bowel (picture a straight line running through an undulating line). This is as horrifying as it sounds. When that happens, we are forced to go in surgically, often having to make multiple incisions in the intestine to access, cut, and remove the string at several points. I suspected Buttercup's family wouldn't be able to afford surgery; they had expressed concern about the cost of the examination when they phoned seeking advice on getting her to eat. They had to be persuaded to bring her in.

Fortunately, sedation is relatively inexpensive, and I didn't need to charge anything extra to cut the string. The string was tense and was biting into the frenulum (the band of tissue at the base of the tongue) so I assumed it was quite long, with both ends extending all the way down the esophagus, through the stomach, and into the intestines. The intestines were playing tug-of-war with the tongue, and neither side was winning. Once I snipped it, it shot down out of sight, like it was in a tremendous hurry to go somewhere.

I walked up to the waiting room and gave the girl and her dad the thumbs up.

"It worked! She should start eating right away. Now we'll just have to watch for the string to come out."

The girl clapped her hands and said, "Yay!"

"But I need to warn you about one thing." I crouched down to get at eye level with the girl. "You might see the end of the string start dangling out of Buttercup's bum. If that happens, don't pull on it!"

The girl looked at me with eyes as wide as loonies and nodded solemnly.

This story has a happy ending. I called the family a few days later to check up on Buttercup and was told that she had indeed passed two pieces of string with no trouble. I spoke to the mom and she thought the string had come from one of innumerable craft kits the kids had. We agreed that children's crafts and a tidy home are entirely incompatible concepts. A week later I received a crayon drawing of Buttercup in the mail. I swear she drew the string hanging out of the hind end, although a colleague tried to persuade me that the line in question was part of the background. But I knew Buttercup's best friend, and I knew better.

THAT BEGGING FACE

The most common abnormal finding during annual physical examinations is the weight (teeth are the second most common). It's so common that the word "abnormal" feels odd. Way too many pets are way too fat.

It's that begging face that's made them that way.

Ask anyone who doesn't believe in evolution to compare how a wolf looks at you when you have food with how a dog looks at you when you have food. It's easy to imagine how the first ancient wolves figured out the right facial expression to be fed scraps from the campfire. Narrow your eyes, flatten your ears, and snarl, and you get chased away. Widen your eyes, relax your ears, and pant, and just maybe you'll hear, "Hey, look at this one! He looks friendly! I'm going to toss him a bone."

Eventually the friendliest-looking wolves had no need to go out and hunt. Begging from humans in exchange for some guarding services was a much better gig. The friendlier they were, the longer they were kept, the more they were bred to pass on those traits. Zoom ahead some 10 or 20 millennia, and dogs now outnumber wolves 5,000 to 1. It worked.

In 1959 Russian scientists Dmitri Belyaev and Lyudmila Trut began an experiment with wild silver foxes to see how rapidly a species could be domesticated using these principles. Year after year, they only bred the least nervous and most friendly of each generation. Friendly tail-wagging was already evident by 1963 and by the end of the long-running experiment in 1999, not only had their behaviour changed radically, but the physical appearance of the foxes had changed as well. The domesticated foxes had gradually begun to look more dog-like, taking on features people find appealing. The foxes had become experts at putting on that begging face.

Orbit, my Shetland sheepdog, has also become an expert. Although he had an adorable face right from the beginning, he had to work on his technique. In the beginning he would bark at us when we were eating dinner. This got him banished to a corner. Eventually he learned that just lying quietly and staring at one of us with his eyes bright and his most winning doggie smile was a far better strategy. We rewarded this, and the absence of barking, with a small dog treat given in his food bowl at the end of the meal. This is the correct response. However, I'm not here to cast stones at those of you who occasionally feed table scraps. Our house is of the thinnest glass in that regard. Somehow that begging face eventually convinced us to give him a few spaghetti noodles, or several, or a spoonful of rice, or a couple spoonfuls, or some leftover carrots, or a handful, instead of the single small dog treat. Sigh. He's not fat yet, but if we keep this up, the trajectory is clear. The law of incrementalism rules. The teensy-tiny increases in what he is given feel irrelevant day by day, but they keep resetting the baseline. I estimate that we're only a year away from setting a place for him at the table. He'd need a special chair, though.

What about cats? Cats are, as you might expect, different. Very different. They sort of have a begging face, but only sort of. Most cats use meowing and rubbing against our legs instead. This seems to work well for them, although I'd like to see the statistics on the number of cats and cooks injured in the process. I can't tell you how often I've tripped over Lucy as she winds around my legs while I'm cooking. It's only luck that has prevented one or both of us being impaled by a carving knife or drenched with a scalding fluid. And yelling, "Goddammit Lucy! Stop it! I'm not giving you anything!" doesn't work. Her strategy seems to be based more on the assurance that her behaviour will increase the chances that I will accidentally drop something. So, not really begging, but pestering and confounding.

Vets and their staff have a colourful vocabulary to describe fat pets. There are blimp-cats and tick-dogs (picture a wood tick with a tiny head and a big, bloated body). There are spheri-cats and chunko-dogs. Many metaphors are deployed as well. A cat or small-sized canine porker may be referred to as a "football" or a "butterball," whereas a medium-sized chubster is invariably a "footstool" and the larger ones are "coffee tables." This is always with an affectionate or, at worst, gently chiding tone, but I wanted you to be aware that your fat pet probably has an unflattering nickname at the vet's. The pets don't care, but you might, and I apologize that this is happening behind your back. We understand that begging face though, so we're not judging. (Much.)

So, what to do? The most common barrier is the misconception many people have regarding the power of exercise. Not a day goes by where I don't hear, "But he gets lots of walks!" Please don't misunderstand and stop exercising your dogs — it's still extremely important for their health — but it is only a minor part of any weight control plan.

Here's a shocking bit of math. The average 10-kilogram (22-pound) dog will burn about 60 calories on a one-hour walk at a 6 kilometres per hour (3.8 miles per hour) pace.* That is, incidentally, pretty darn fast. With all his sniffing, Orbit is closer to 4 kilometres per hour. Now here's the shocking part: a medium-sized Milk Bone has 40 calories. So, depending on your dog's size and pace, he may need to walk an hour or more to burn the calories in one medium-sized Milk Bone. Think about that when he deploys that begging face. And that's not to pick on Milk Bones (although while we're on the subject, they do not have the advertised benefits for the teeth). The great majority of commercial dog treats are high-calorie. It makes sense, doesn't it? They are "treats," after all, and people like to see their dogs enjoy them. Dogs love rich things just the way we do. But fortunately, they also just love food in

---

*   To convert this to your own dog's weight, it works out to 1.1 calories per kg of dog per km walked, or 0.8 calories per pound of dog per mile walked.

general, so you can often get away with giving a bit of fruit or vegetable instead, and many (although not all) dogs will be delighted. A slice of raw carrot has one calorie.

We cannot resist that begging face, and the ancient bond first forged around a campfire a thousand generations ago needs to be honoured. Just honour it with fewer calories.

THUD

I've seen it happen at least a dozen times, probably more. The first time was in veterinary school during our first surgery lab, and since then it's always been in the operating room at the clinic with a volunteer or student. And once I didn't see it, I just heard it: thud. She hit the floor. In case you haven't figured it out yet, I'm talking about people fainting at the sight of blood. The technical term for this is vasovagal syncope. Don't worry, I'll explain.

When I don't have oblivious tunnel-vision focus on some aspect of the surgery, I will usually pick up on the warning signs and suggest that the individual sit down or step out to get a glass of water. Typically, they look a little pale and are starting to sweat. If they had been chatty before they suddenly become quiet and have a distant, unfocused look in their eyes. Sometimes they are unaware of what's about to happen and will say, "Oh no, I'm fine, thanks. It's just a little warm in here." No, it's not. Okay, sometimes it is, but not over where the person is standing, well away from the surgery light. No, that warm feeling, and maybe a touch of nausea, and, curiously enough, sometimes yawning, are all signs that you are about to faint. The floor is extremely hard and it's a long way down from the perspective of your head. So, listen to the nice doctor and sit down, or leave for a few minutes. It happens to all ages, all genders, and all backgrounds. But one thing that unites the blood fainters is embarrassment. And that's too bad because it's nothing to be embarrassed about. None of us who see this happen judge these poor people in any way.

But why does it happen? It turns out that it's genetic and roughly 15% of the population is prone to fainting when exposed to blood. The theory is that this may actually be an evolutionary advantage. How so? An early push to the health benefits of vegetarianism? No, the thought is that during battles, those who fainted had an advantage because they would be assumed to be dead and therefore left alone by the enemy. This strikes me as a dubious strategy, and an even more dubious theory — why wouldn't non-fainters just start pretending to faint more often if that worked so well? I'm picturing two tribes of cavemen rushing at each other, waving spears and clubs, screaming at the top of their lungs, and then they all simultaneously drop to the ground except one or two keeners who wander around looking bewildered. Or perhaps most of them *were* keeners? Anyway, clearly the theory needs work, but it's a cute idea.

At the start I said it happened to one of my classmates. You must be wondering how that person managed in practice. She managed just fine. She's an excellent veterinarian now. Anxiety can significantly raise the risk of this happening, and performing your first surgery ever under the beady-eyed gaze of your professor is, I can assure you, a cause for anxiety. It gets better.

And there are also techniques you can learn to reduce the risk. Remember when I called it "vasovagal syncope"? That means that the blood vessels are dilating in your extremities, drawing blood away from your brain. And when your brain doesn't get enough blood, you pass out. Therefore, doctors recommend the "applied tension technique" whereby you learn to tense the muscles in your limbs, thereby raising blood pressure and countering the vessel dilation. Over time this becomes a reflex, and the problem goes away.

I tell this story in the hope that it will reach one or two people who want to become veterinarians but assume their reaction to blood precludes the possibility. It doesn't necessarily. Don't let a little vasovagal syncope get between you and your dreams.

The same goes for most of the other fears and qualms that seem like insurmountable obstacles. You can't stand bad smells? You get used to it. You can't stand the sight of gross things like pus or parasites or guts? You get used to it. You can't stand the thought of having to tell people their pet is going to die? You don't get used to that, but you do learn how to do it in a way that doesn't devastate you every time.

Something that can, however, get in the way of your dreams is anaphylaxis. I had another classmate who developed a severe, life-threatening allergic reaction to horse dander in first year of veterinary school. You can avoid horses in your professional life, but you cannot avoid them in your training. He had to drop out, which I'm sure broke his heart.

I can never tell on meeting a new student or volunteer who's going to swoon and who isn't, so there's no way to screen for it, but we have learned to keep an extra stool handy in the operating room.

TO ERR

I make mistakes. You make mistakes. Your mother makes mistakes. The Queen makes mistakes. The Pope makes mistakes. My dog and my cats make mistakes, although I doubt they would ever admit it. The point is that everyone makes mistakes. For obvious reasons, it is, however, particularly alarming when a doctor makes a mistake. Consequently, we have all sorts of systems and double-checks in place to reduce the number of mistakes. Nonetheless, you'll note the use of the word "reduce," not "eliminate" — mistakes still happen. They are rare and, thankfully, I can't recall making a fatal one, but they still happen.

Even our regulations recognize the reality of human error. Disciplinary complaints based on an isolated mistake are generally dismissed. This is not to deny the harm that mistakes can cause, but to recognize that it is unavoidable that some will occur. Nonetheless, I'm sure we can all agree that we should aim for as few as humanly possible. Fortunately, the whole subject of medical errors is becoming a hot topic. On a quick search, I found over 20 books recently published on this. This is a good thing, because open conversation about the reality of mistakes makes them feel slightly less shameful. Veterinarians tend towards being neurotic introverts, so it is easy for individuals to believe that they are the only ones making mistakes and therefore feel compelled to hide those mistakes. But acknowledging the reality that all of your colleagues, even the ones you admire most, goof up from time to time makes it easier to fess up to your own missteps and thereby permit everyone to learn from them.

So, all that said, in the spirit of fessing up, here is my latest whopper. One of the receptionists had handed me a refill request for Ralphie Erikson's ongoing prescription of Enalapril. This is a blood pressure medication that is often used in heart disease. Ralphie was a decrepit old Pomeranian and most decrepit old Pomeranians have heart issues, so no surprise there. I scrolled through his file and saw that the meds had been filled about a half-dozen times since somebody last spoke to Mr. Erikson. I was confused, though, because it is unusual to use Enalapril by itself. Most often it's paired with a diuretic. There are exceptions in the earliest stages of heart disease, but I couldn't find reference to that in the record. His chart was very lengthy, though, so I'll confess to scanning it more than actually reading it. Regardless, it was clear that it had been a long time since Ralphie had been in, so I decided to give Mr. Erikson a quick call.

"I see there's a refill request here, I just wanted to check how Ralphie's doing first."

"Thanks for calling, Doc. He's great, but he's pretty itchy."

I was confused. Itchiness was not an expected side effect. "So, he's been itchy since you started the meds you mean?"

"No, that was his main symptom before and then it got better for a while and now it's worse again."

Now I was even more confused, so I improvised. "Ah, well, that is unusual. You know what? Let me look into this and I'll get back to you. It's okay to be off the Enalapril for now, so let's not fill that if it's not working until I can figure something else out. Okay?"

"That sounds great. Thanks for calling!"

I hung up and stared at the phone for a long moment. This made no sense whatsoever. Fortunately, my next appointment had cancelled when they couldn't catch their cat, so I had a few minutes to carefully read through Ralphie's file. There were no references to heart problems, not even a murmur, which was almost bizarre in an elderly

Pom, but he had been diagnosed with seasonal allergies. The Eriksons have four dogs, all of them Pomeranians, all of them old. I vaguely remembered that one of them had allergies, but I thought it was Bingly. (Hey, stop judging, I see well over a thousand different patients every year!)

Uh-oh.

I dug a little further and, sure enough, six months ago I had intended to prescribe Apoquel, not Enalapril. I had written "Apoquel" in my notes, but somehow Enalapril was dispensed. And the heart medication had been refilled in the intervening months several times by my colleagues and by myself.

Whoopsie daisy.

Fortunately Enalapril is relatively harmless, and fortunately allergies aren't life threatening and Ralphie's were relatively mild, so no harm done, except to my peace of mind. I felt my stomach tighten and my skin crawl. Oh my god. This could have been so much worse. But it was bad enough. How could this have happened? Did I verbally say "Apoquel" to the receptionist and she heard "Enalapril?" I suppose they almost rhyme, but they don't really sound that similar. It's not like the more understandable confusion between Convenia and Cerenia, or Benazapril and Benadryl. Did I write a prescription, but have a brain fart, and write the wrong drug name? For those of you with a joke about doctor's handwriting at the tip of your tongue, it's all typed now, so I don't even have that inexcusable excuse. The "half a pill, once a day" instructions happen coincidentally to be the same, so maybe that's where wires got crossed?

Regardless, it was a mistake, and it was a bad mistake that was compounded by the fact that multiple doctors (including me!) reapproved this prescription without catching the original error. It's only through good fortune that it didn't have any significant consequences for the patient.

Ralphie's itch is under control now and Mr. Erikson was very understanding when I told him that I had accidentally been sending the wrong drug home. Alexander Pope said that to err is human, but to forgive is divine. I think to forgive is exceptionally human as well. Thank you, Mr. Erikson.

VETERINARY VOCABULARY MISCELLANY

This is for you Scrabble fans out there. I don't play much Scrabble myself, so I don't know how valuable these words are, but hopefully there's at least one that wows your opponents. For the rest of you, this is just a little toe-dip into the ocean of veterinary words. It stretches to the horizon and is deeper than you dare imagine. I know you're thinking, "Oh great, here comes a bunch of polysyllabic Latin obscurities you white-coaters spout to make yourselves sound smart." Ugh. No, that would be too easy. This is a miscellany of other odd veterinary

words.[*] I decided to write this when I ran across a column by Ben Schott, who is the author of *Schott's Original Miscellany*, a marvellous volume stuffed full of weird facts, lists, trivia, and nuggets of wisdom. We're

---

[*] A clarification: many of these words are not exclusively veterinary but are shared with human medicine or are zoological in origin, but they are all words I learned during my training.

not related, but there may be something about Schotts that attracts them to this sort of thing.

BORBORYGMUS

This is fun to say. Try it! Any idea what it means? It sounds like a dance to me, although that probably says more about me as a dancer than it does about "borborygmus" as a word. It's the squirty and rumbly sounds the stomach and intestines make as they do their thing. Listening for borborygmus is something of an obsession in large animal medicine. In small animal medicine we are more likely to use the word to confuse or intimidate students.

CARNASSIAL

If your dog or cat is nearby, grab them (gently) and lift their lips near the corner of the mouth. That really big tooth at the top? Yes, the biggest one. That's the carnassial. Technically, it's the fourth premolar. Its opposite number on the bottom is the first molar. They meet in a scissor-like fashion to shear through meat. It's a big part of what makes a carnivore a carnivore. They don't shear through rocks quite as well, so they are also the most commonly broken teeth in dogs (see below).

CLINGON

Putting a smile on the face of any Trekkie, this refers to a dried chunk of poop clinging to the fur around a pet's bum.

CRIA

A baby llama, and arguably the cutest baby animal anywhere. One was hospitalized with a broken pastern (see
below) while I was in vet school. Picture a golden retriever–
sized llama with dense, luxuriant mahogany brown fur, giant
shining black eyes, and improbably long black eyelashes, like
an anime cartoon. Students lined up to hug the cria. This is
ironic because adult llamas are among the least huggable species. Not only do they spit (incidentally, this is a euphemism;
it's actually vomit) on you, but people have been injured and
even killed when chest-butted by angry males.

FLEHMEN

Have you ever seen a horse curl back his upper lip, exposing
his gums and top teeth? This is called the flehmen response.
Other animals do it too, including occasionally cats. It
makes them look angry or demented, but it's a way of drawing air into a little structure called the vomeronasal organ
behind the upper teeth. Various organic compounds, especially pheromones, are analyzed there, usually to tell the
animal something about the reproductive status of another
animal. Imagine if humans were able to flehmen? Awkward.

HOB

A male ferret. I suspect it's no coincidence that "hob"
used to also refer to a sprite, elf, or other mischievous
woodland being.

JILL

A female ferret. This is a particular gift to Scrabble players. My understanding is that some rule sets permit the use of proper names, but many do not. If you are not allowed proper names, you can now play "jill" and be all smug about it when your opponent challenges you.

MELENA

Nope, not the former First Lady of the United States. Good guess. It refers to black tarry feces resulting from digested blood.

PASTERN

The sloping part of a horse's foot between the hoof and the first obvious joint (called the fetlock — consider that a bonus word). It consists of two bones that in you and me are the last two fingers or toe bones. The whole lower leg of a horse is a single elongated toe. It stands on its toenails. Llamas have pasterns too (see above), as do cows, rhinos, giraffes, and all the other ungulates (meaning hoofed animals — second bonus word).

PICA

Eating non-food items, especially rocks and soil. Wild animals may do it to correct mineral deficiencies. Our pets do it because they are foolish. Sometimes this breaks their carnassial teeth (see above).

QIVIUT

Muskox wool. It's reputedly the softest and warmest wool in the world. One of my favourite professors in vet school, Dr. Peter Flood, studied muskoxen with the intent of helping the Inuit manage muskox for a commercial qiviut industry. In the Canadian Arctic, most qiviut was gathered by finding places where wild muskoxen had shed and rubbed their wool off on rocks, or by hunting them. Consequently, we had a few of the impressively large and hairy animals in a robust enclosure behind the vet college buildings. To my regret, I never got to touch one and could only view them from a safe remove.

STIFLE

The Scrabble players, stifling a yawn, are thinking that this isn't a new word. I suppose it isn't, but it's a completely new use for it. A stifle is what we call an animal's knee, especially in a dog or cat. People are frequently confused about where, exactly, their pet's knee is. They will sometimes point to the ankle or to something on the front leg. Dogs and cats stand on their toes, so the first joint you see in the back leg is the ankle. It points backwards. The stifle, or knee, is the first joint that points forwards, just like in your leg. Incidentally, a sizable majority of mammals stand on their toes. Humans are the freaks in this regard.

WETHER

A castrated ram. This allows you to say, "Do you know whether the wether weathers well?"

XYLITOL

Xylitol is a ubiquitous sugar substitute, and it is highly poisonous in dogs. Cats are not affected. (But they have lilies to worry about.) It can cause the dog's blood sugar to plunge, putting them into a life-threatening hypoglycemic crisis, and it can severely damage the liver. Almost all sugar-free gum has xylitol in it, and many over-the-counter children's medicines do too.

I'm sorry, that wasn't a particularly fun note to end on. But it was an important fact that I wanted to work in somewhere. I'll make it up to you in the next story.

WHAT A PICTURE IS WORTH

According to the cliché, a thousand words. Often this is

true. But sometimes it isn't. Sometimes a picture is worth far fewer words. Take, for example, a picture a client emailed to me the other day. That one was worth only three words: "What the heck?" (I might have said something slightly different, but it was still only three words.)

The client had sent me a close-up picture of their dog's anus.

No explanation. Nothing in the subject line. Just a photo of the anus. Was there a problem with the anus? Or was this some sort of weird postmodern insult?

Since the beginning of the pandemic, we've been encouraging clients with non-urgent concerns to reach out to us by telephone or email. Some issues can be resolved this way, without having to see the animal. Occasionally a photo is helpful too, so I may ask the client to send me a picture to show me how big something is, or how red it is, or exactly where it is. But it's rare to be able to make a diagnosis from a picture alone. It's just another piece of evidence. It's a little like a criminal investigation. How many times is a detective able to solve a case just by looking at a crime scene photo? Every now and again, but not often.

The other limitation of photos is their — I'll put this politely — variable quality. The ubiquity of cellphone cameras has greatly increased the convenience and ease of photography, but it has done nothing to increase the skill of the average photographer. Many pictures that land in my inbox are blurry or dark or washed out or shot from a bizarre angle. For example, a common photo is of a pink smudge on some unidentified part of the pet's skin.

I suppose that could be a rash, or a bruise, or lipstick . . . There's no way to tell. Another example is the flash-lit photo of a pet's eyeball. I can see the photographer in the curved funhouse reflection, but not much else. Or the all-time classic: the blurry lump. I probably get one of those a day. Yup, there's something pinkish protruding through the fur. That's about all I can say.

In rereading the preceding paragraph, I realize that I might have come across as mean and snarky. Some of you are probably squirming in embarrassment at the memory of a suboptimal photo you once sent to your veterinarian. I apologize! I know you are doing your best, and that your flawed photo is in fact a compliment to your veterinarian. You are so confident in their diagnostic prowess that you assume even a poor photograph will be enough to nail the diagnosis for them. We veterinarians often seem to have weird and arcane powers of deduction, so it's a worth a try. Please don't worry; we do appreciate the effort and the vote of confidence. Just be aware that we will probably still need to see the pet in person.

And even a perfect picture does not always help. Many kinds of lumps are identical in appearance, as are many different eye conditions, skin diseases, and, well, anal complaints.

This anus was, for the record, perfectly in focus, nicely centred, and beautifully lit. It was an exceptionally high-quality photograph. Very impressive. But I was still bewildered. And this, finally, brings me to my main point, which is that history is key. We need the picture *and* the thousand words. Or at least a dozen. Was he licking at his bum? Rubbing it on the carpet? How long has he been doing this? Was something unexpected coming out of the anus that wasn't captured in the photo? Was the anus doing something strange? Don't laugh — my colleague once received a video clip featuring a dog's anus winking. It was just a muscle spasm and nothing to worry about, but the owners had never seen anything like that before and were a little alarmed. My colleague continued to play it full-screen on a loop for a little while, to the general merriment of passersby in the office.

So, I wrote back. I thanked the client for the lovely photo and asked what their concern was. A while later the reply came that he was, in fact, licking at his hind end. They hoped there was something there that had attracted his attention that they couldn't see, but I would be able to. I thanked them for their faith in my powers, but said I was forced to confess that it looked normal to me as well. I then explained that there are several possible reasons for bum licking. The most common among these would be the anal sacs being full. For the uninitiated, these are a pair of scent glands on either side of the anus. We would have to see him to know for sure. He would need a rectal examination.

They made the appointment and, sure enough, a quick lubricated feel confirmed the full sacs. The dog, a small brown Heinz 57 named Bernie, was remarkably untroubled by this intrusion and I was quickly able to resolve the issue with a gentle emptying squeeze.

In this case, it was a finger that was worth a thousand words.

WHAT'S BROWN AND STICKY?

A stick. What did you think I was going to say?

I apologize — it's an old joke and kind of a terrible one — but if you have any kids around who haven't heard it before, try it on them. It'll crack them up. *Guar-an-teed*.

I was thinking about this joke early today when I was taking a walk on the banks of the Assiniboine River west of my house and encountered a corgi carrying a stick the size of a small tree in his mouth. Corgis are already front-heavy, so I wasn't sure how he was managing this without tipping forward. Perhaps his owners had taped lead weights to his hips, but as I walked past him, I couldn't see any. In any case, he looked absolutely delighted. Absurd, but delighted. Have you ever noticed this? The happiest dogs are the ones carrying sticks. And if the sight of a happy dog carrying a stick doesn't gladden your heart, then what are you doing with this book in your hands? (Okay, unless you're a hardcore cat person and were sucked in by the book's title.)

The advisability and safety of dogs chewing sticks is one of the most common questions asked of veterinarians.

Many dogs not only pick up sticks and carry them around like an accessory, but also chew on them and even eat them, swallowing slivers and chunks. Surely this must be bad for them, right?

Wrong. Mostly wrong.

Orbit is also a stick chewer, or rather I should say a twig eater. He's uninterested in true sticks, preferring finger-sized twigs, and he eats them — crunch, crunch, swallow. Using criteria that are imperceptible to the human observer, he carefully inspects twig after twig before selecting the one that suits his tastes. He has the discernment of a wine aficionado. You could say that he is a twig connoisseur. And then, as I mentioned, he eats it. This has no ill effect. In fact, over all the years I've been in practice, I have surgically removed all manner of foreign objects ranging from socks to rocks to coins to toys from animal's stomachs, but never once a stick or any piece of wood. They seem to be able to digest them. It stands to reason that if they overindulge in sticks, diarrhea might result from the heavy fibre load, but I haven't even seen that.

(Be assured that by the time you have read this, a couple of my colleagues have already contacted me to tell me about the time they had a patient who couldn't digest a stick and had problems. But it's rare. Struck-by-lightning rare.)

There are a couple of caveats, though. The first is that some things that kind of look like little twigs are not and are dangerous. Specifically, coconut husk mulch (also called coir) and cocoa hull mulch can cause problems. The former can absorb so much water in the digestive tract that it expands to cause a blockage, while the latter contains enough chocolate essence to be toxic.

The other caveat was brought to light a couple of years ago when a young couple came in with their golden retriever, Stella, frantic that she was having some sort of seizure or fit.

Sure enough, Stella was shaking her head, pawing at her mouth, and drooling profusely. She had a wild look in her eyes and was clearly in distress.

You have an advantage over me. You have a pretty good idea of what is going on with Stella because we've been discussing stick chewing. But I had no clue. On first glance, Stella's symptoms were bizarre, although it obviously had something to do with the mouth, at least in part. I guessed she might have broken a tooth, but the reaction seemed extreme for that. She wouldn't let me open her mouth. She just kept pulling her head away. After a few minutes of fruitless attempts, and just before I was going to suggest sedation, she opened her mouth a little to pant and I got a split-second glance.

There was a stick jammed across the roof of her mouth between her upper molars.

This was easy to fix, or at least it was once I settled her with a mild sedative. The owners were so relieved. But that's the only time one of my patients has had a medical problem due to chewing on a stick. Quite a few of them have cut and even impaled themselves on sharp sticks running through the woods, but that's a different category of problem entirely.

Incidentally, Stella's situation reminds me of a case one of my colleagues recently saw. This time it was a small hairy dog, a shih tzu, I think. She was so hairy that from a distance you could only tell the front end from the back end by the fact that the front end stuck out from the legs a little more. She was old and had, according to the owners, suddenly begun to seize and run in circles. It was sad, but it was clearly her time. When they came in for the euthanasia my colleague noticed that the dog's front right leg wasn't visible. This was probably related to why she kept turning in tight circles to the right. Moreover, her "seizures" involved rapid jerking on the right side.

The vet had a careful look and discovered that a claw from the right forepaw had gotten hooked in a mat by the right ear.

It was a miracle! Her owners were as relieved as Stella's were. After a nail trim and a grooming, the old girl went on to live another year.

Let's finish with another joke for the kids. Why don't dogs make good dancers? Because they have two left feet!

YOU STINK

No, not you (presumably at least). It's me. I stink or, more accurately, I stank. I don't anymore. Not most of the time anyway. Back in vet school I stank, and people told me so. They said, "You stink." Hence the title of this story. But this was not due to any deficiency in personal hygiene. I may have sported a cheesy little moustache and I may have had a limited wardrobe, but I did wash and shower daily. No, I stank because of my part-time job. During first and second year of vet school I looked after a research mink colony. It was my job to feed and water them and report any obvious health issues to the graduate student in charge of the study. It turns out that mink are ideal subjects for studying the hormone melatonin and it also turns out that mink stink. It rhymes, and it's true.

Mink belong to the "mustelid" family of carnivores that includes ferrets, weasels, otters, badgers, and wolverines. A number of features unite this family, but the one most relevant to this story is that they all are equipped with infamously pungent anal scent glands. Pet ferrets routinely have these surgically removed at a young age. Research mink do not, so a pen with 30 mink in individual cages smells like all the locker rooms of all the teenage boys' junior hockey teams in Canada compressed and distilled into a space the size of the average living room. Mink tolerate cold very well, even Saskatchewan cold, so fortunately the pen was outdoors. An enclosed space would have been lethal. But nonetheless, the stench was eye-watering, literally. And it rapidly permeated everything — my clothing, my hair, my skin even.

And that's only the first reason I stank.

The second reason was what I fed the mink. Their diet consisted of a horrifying purée of leftover chicken bits. I would bring them this pinkish slop by the bucketload. Beaks, feathers, and claws were suspended in it, like raisins in Satan's own version of breakfast porridge. I had to carry these buckets quite a distance, so inevitably some of it sloshed onto my coveralls. From November onwards these chunks froze instantly into place.

For most of our classes we were sorted into two groups alphabetically by last name. This put a pretty, petite brunette named Lorraine Walker in my group. I had thus far had a woeful romantic life, but things were looking up in vet school, where the female-to-male ratio was over two to one. Lorraine had caught my eye and we'd exchanged a few words, but she was usually with her Manitoba clique and rarely had a free seat beside her. That is until one day when, fresh from the mink pens with no time to change out of my coveralls, I saw my chance. The seat to her right was open. I sat down and said, "Hi!" She smiled and said hi back. That's when I saw it. There was a whole chicken beak frozen in place on my left thigh. I thought about trying to flick it away, but that would only attract attention to it. Moreover, I was worried I would end up accidentally sending it into someone's hair in the next row.

"Doing something in the large animal ward?" she asked, looking at my grimy coveralls, but thankfully not appearing to notice the beak, or the stench.

"No, I have a job feeding mink for Dr. Bruce Murphy. They're out back, towards VIDO."

"Oh," she smiled and nodded and turned back to her notebook. The lecture was beginning.

That went well, I thought.

I started scribbling away in my notebook as well, absorbed in the intricacies of cardiopulmonary physiology. But after only a few minutes the pink chicken guck on my coveralls began thawing, adding a certain "je ne sais quoi" to the background mink pong that was already emanating from me. And then, to my horror, the beak started sliding down the left side of my leg. Lorraine's bag was right below there.

But Lorraine didn't notice this. She noticed something else. When the professor paused to change transparency rolls on his overhead projector she leaned over, wrinkled her nose, and whispered, "You stink."

But I noticed she was smiling when she said this.

A couple weeks later we went on our first date. And now it's 35 years after that and she still occasionally tells me that I stink, but I never have chicken parts stuck to me anymore.

ZENITH

Let me start with a confession — I selected the title of this story in part because I wanted it to come last and therefore needed it to start with Z. But I think it works. I like the word "zenith." It doesn't get nearly enough use anymore, especially since Zenith stopped making televisions in the late 1990s. But it's due for a comeback as a way to describe the peak of something — the opposite of rock bottom, or nadir.

Perhaps the zenith of my career is still to come, but if it's right now, then I'll be satisfied too, because right now is good, and the moment encapsulates one of the most positive aspects of being a small animal veterinarian.

Veterinarians are a grumblier and more cynical bunch than you might imagine. Get a group of them together and you can't finish mixing a proper cocktail in the time it takes for one of them to move from pleasantries to launching into complaining about clients, or staff, or equipment, or drug companies, or how busy they are, or how stressed they are, or how unappreciated they feel. And on it goes. Consequently, I rarely get a group of veterinarians together. I love them, and they are "my people" much in the way soldiers or kindergarten teachers or other misunderstood professionals automatically bond with each other, but there's a limit.

I can complain right along with the best of them, but one aspect of practice I keep reminding myself not to complain about is the clients. Interaction after interaction has taught me that 99% of pet owners who come to the clinic are good people. Okay, okay, let's say 98%. This has been the most profound thing I have learned in over 30 years, well ahead of any medical fact or surgical procedure. I'm not saying that clients are always easy to deal with and I may not always agree with their decisions, but at their core I can see that they are good and that they mean well. Unfortunately, it is human nature to focus on the 2% who are exceptions to this rule. We wouldn't do that with books, or movies, or meals — if 98% of them were good, we'd be so delighted that we would completely forget about the other 2%. But human interaction is obviously much more personal, so the negative sticks.

But I am lucky because it seems to stick a little less to me. Year after year, as I get to know more people, my satisfaction with my choice of profession increases. What happened today helps to confirm for me that I may be at the zenith. It's not that I think it's going to start careening downhill from here, but I just don't see how it can improve any further. The zenith is hopefully a long high plateau, not a pointy little peak.

So, here's what happened today.

I found out today that a client wants to make an anonymous donation to Birchwood Animal Hospital. Donations are not unheard of, but the amount was. $5,000 may not sound like much to people in the human field who routinely deal with multi-million-dollar bequests, but believe me when I say that for us, it is astonishingly generous. It is an order of magnitude greater than any donation we have received before. She wants us to use it to buy something for the practice, perhaps a piece of equipment to enhance patient care that we've always wanted, but which never quite made it into the budget.

This little anecdote illustrates my point about the goodness of people, or pet owners at least. Of course, this is just one person, but she is emblematic of the respect we have in the community as veterinarians. Most people couldn't afford that sort of donation, and I'm sure others view the relationship as strictly transactional and would no more donate to a vet clinic than they would tip their lawyer, but regardless, the great majority of our clients want us to do well. When we do well, then we are better able to help their animals, which in turn improves the client's own lives, and then they appreciate us even more. It is a virtuous circle.

Please do not see this as a call for more donations! They are in no way necessary. The smiles and thank-yous that most of you (98% of you) are already giving us are more than sufficient. We veterinarians just need to do a better job of noticing and appreciating them.

I know that Murphy's Law — and, for you fellow math geeks, regression to the mean — suggest that tomorrow could be a disaster with crises erupting and patients crashing and clients screaming and staff flailing, but if so, approaching it from the zenith of my career will take the sting out.

EPILOGUE

THE SENTIMENTAL VETERINARIAN

Occasionally I will find myself alone in the clinic at the end of an evening shift. The busy sounds of the clinic being put back into order eventually cease and the murmur of staff chatting amongst themselves about their evening plans fades as they walk to the back door. Then there are distant shouts of "We're going now!" and "Good night, Philipp!" And then there is silence. We rarely hospitalize animals overnight anymore as critical patients are better off being transferred to a hospital with 24-hour staffing and most of the other ones are better off at home, so the clinic is usually completely empty after the staff leave. When I'm still there, it's because I've got files to write on, or cases to research, or clients to call. Most of the time when all that work is done, I'm eager to get home, so I will grab my coat, turn off the office light, go directly to the back door, lock up, and leave. But every now and again I find myself in a reflective, sentimental mood, and I wander around the clinic for a while first.

As I go past the dark, silent exam rooms, images of patients and clients and staff come to mind. I might think about Earl, the enormous German shepherd who always viewed me with deepest suspicion and who, honestly, frightened me a little, but whose owner was very nice and really liked me and refused to see anybody else, so Earl and I had to deal with each other for his entire life. He never tried to bite me, but in my heart, I know that he thought about it all the time.

Or I might picture that litter of kittens a week ago that we couldn't tell apart until we made little coloured neck bands. All kittens are cute, of course, but these were especially cute, and the exam room became host to a parade of staff coming to coo and cuddle.

Or I might remember Suzie, the 21-year-old cat I put to sleep earlier in the day. She was so frail that I thought the sedation I gave before the euthanasia injection might be enough on its own, but in the manner of so many ancient cats, she was almost supernaturally tough and kept right on breathing, and even purring, until the very last fraction of the euthanasia solution flowed into her system.

Or I might think about Mr. Albertson and his two little Lhasa Apsos, Lizzie and Betty, and how when he developed liver cancer his biggest concern was who would look after the dogs. He was one of the gentlest, kindest men I have ever met. I thought about going to his funeral. I still regret that I didn't.

And then, as I walk past Bob's picture at the edge of the waiting room, I think about him, my partner in this practice up until a dozen years ago when he passed away. Tales of some of his quirks have woven themselves into the practice lore, so that staff who have never met him know who he is, even if their image of him belongs more to the legend than to the man. I still miss the man.

The next stop is the reception desk and another bittersweet memory. This was Heather's domain, our head receptionist for many years. She is also gone now and is also someone I still miss. We were the same age and had the same cultural references — '80s music, Monty Python, *Star Wars*. Now everyone is younger, often much younger.

But this is not just a visit with the ghosts of Birchwood. On these evenings I will often stand for a long moment in the empty waiting room and marvel at the contrast to a few hours prior when it hosted a cacophony of dogs and cats and birds and clients and staff and ringing telephones. The sensation is akin to that of standing in a dry riverbed. The mental echo of the river's powerful tumult is so strong that its absence feels eerie and unnatural. It makes me smile to think about how much life is normally here, and how intense that life often is. This is a place where so many emotions are strongly felt and so many intersect. Yes, this can be stressful, but overriding that is the wonderful feeling of being in the midst of the life of your community — in the surging current, paddling, shouting, laughing, screaming, crying along with everyone else. Not just watching from the bank.

I am a sentimental veterinarian. To be sure, I spend a lot of time thinking about the practicalities of my cases, and the science behind them, but I spend an equal amount of time thinking about my past and present patients and clients and staff not just as patients and clients and staff, but as multi-dimensional individuals with deeply interesting lives and stories. As real animals and as real people. I love this about my job. This is life. This is veterinary medicine.

Acknowledgements

The writer gets all the credit, all the praise, and if there is any actual glory, all of that too. The truth, however, is that this book would not exist if it weren't for a long line of other people. At the head of this line are my editors, Jack David and Cat London, and not far behind are the illustrator, Brian Gable, and the cover designer, David Gee. But the line snakes on through the ECW Press office and their brilliant publicists, marketing and design specialists, production editors, audiobook coordinators, marketing managers, art directors, digital directors, and I'm sure the list goes on. This is my fifth book, and the process still feels deliciously mysterious, so my apologies if I've missed anyone in the office. And what about the printers, truck drivers, warehouse workers, librarians, and booksellers? Without any of them, this book would be sitting forlornly on a hard drive in the ECW office, gathering digital dust, feeling pointless and sad.

And then there's the other line, the even longer one. That's the line of my clients with their pets beside them. Picture all of them, the line snaking well past the horizon. There are thousands upon thousands. Assuming the animals all get along, it makes for a nice visual, doesn't it? They all need to be acknowledged and thanked as well. Without them, there would be no book. It's that simple.

Finally, there's a little circle of my family, my own pets, and my friends. Without them, there would be no book either. They give me the space, the energy, the encouragement, and sometimes the inspiration.

Between these lines and circles it's quite a crowd. Some say writing is lonely work. I disagree.

This book is also available as a Global Certified Accessible™ (GCA) ebook. ECW Press's ebooks are screen reader friendly and are built to meet the needs of those who are unable to read standard print due to blindness, low vision, dyslexia, or a physical disability.

At ECW Press, we want you to enjoy our books in whatever format you like. If you've bought a print copy just send an email to ebook@ecwpress.com and include:

- the book title
- the name of the store where you purchased it
- a screenshot or picture of your order/receipt number and your name
- your preference of file type: PDF (for desktop reading), ePub (for a phone/tablet, Kobo, or Nook), mobi (for Kindle)

A real person will respond to your email with your ebook attached. Please note this offer is only for copies bought for personal use and does not apply to school or library copies.

Thank you for supporting an independently owned Canadian publisher with your purchase!

This book is made of paper from well-managed FSC® - certified forests, recycled materials, and other controlled sources.